J. P. Philpott

The Kingdom of Israel

From its Inception under Joshua, its first President, in the Year of the

World 2353, to the second Advent of Christ

J. P. Philpott

The Kingdom of Israel
From its Inception under Joshua, its first President, in the Year of the World 2353, to the second Advent of Christ

ISBN/EAN: 9783337254735

Printed in Europe, USA, Canada, Australia, Japan

Cover: Foto ©ninafisch / pixelio.de

More available books at **www.hansebooks.com**

THE

KINGDOM OF ISRÆL;

From its inception under Joshua, its first President, in the Year
of the World 2353, to the second advent of Christ

CONSIDERED, FIRST, AS TYPICAL UNDER ITS THREE FIRST HEADS,
AND THE UNITED STATES SHOWN TO BE THE THIRD
AND LAST OF THOSE HEADS

Considered: Second, as Antitypical, and the Confeder
ate States shown to be the Grand Antitype in
its first appearance, to ultimate in the
"Throne of the Prince of the House of David."

Dedicated to the Rev. S. D. BALDWIN,

AUTHOR OF "ARMAGEDDON," &C.,

IF LIVING, AND TO HIS MEMORY IF DEAD.

BY J. P. PHILPOTT.

FAIRFIELD, TEXAS:
PIONEER OFFICE PRINT.
MAY, 1861.

PREFACE.

WE come before the public for the first time, never having written even a short newspaper article in life; and in doing so, it may not be amiss for us to state that we were induced to do so from a thorough conviction that there was much written in the Bible of a *strictly political* character, applicable to the past, present and future of our country, that has never been noticed or understood as such. We were impressed with a sense of duty to God, ourselves as a nation, and to mankind in general, to take up the subject of Bible Teachings Politically, and discuss it in a few short notes—noticing a few of the many Prophecies that speak and teach nationally, that apply strictly to modern times, or "latter days" —embracing the rise, progress and fall of the United States of America, and of the rise of three nationalities out of the fallen United States, to ultimate in one; the Confederate States foretold in Prophecy as being the chief of the three, and to absorb the other two, as above intimated : and how and when this Union upon the Confederacy was to be effected, and the present war have an end, &c.

We make no apology for what we have written—claiming the right accorded to all—of free speech. That right, with others, we are now battling for; and as we claim it, we would withhold it from none ; and shall expect that others, in the exercise of that right, may take ground against us upon some points in these notes. If they do not, it will be strange indeed ; for we occupy positions in opposition to " names renowned;" in opposition to tenets "hoar with centuries."

We are well aware that we have not handled the subject as it deserves to be ; nor are our notes more than an introduction to the vast subject. Volumes might and should at once be written upon it, by hands and heads competent to do it full justice. The times have brought us out. Recent scriptural revealment by fulfilment of Prophecy elicited our attention, and a close investigation followed, and these hasty notes are the result. They are very defective as to arrangement and diction : of this, however, the reader need not be told—the fact is patent. The want, in digest, could not well be avoided, for we have jotted down our thoughts, running over a period of twelve months or more, and much of them have been written in camp and on the march, with very little privacy, and sometimes without a Bible for reference, and some of our quotations are given from memory, and may in some instances not be literal, but always retaining the sense. And again, we have not even had time to copy our notes, and with the exception of a few sheets, they now go to press just as we penciled them by the way. As to the diction, it is our own, and just like us—"rough as a rasp."

If these notes shall prove the means, under God, of calling attention to, and inducing a closer and more thorough searching of the scriptures of truth, by those who may read them, I shall be well paid for my toil ; not to say that I am not already a thousand times repaid for my investigation by the satisfaction arising from the sacred truths made plain to my mind.

FAIRFIELD, TEXAS, *May*, 1864.

CHAPTER FIRST:

INTRODUCTION:

DOES God concern Himself about the political or national affairs of earth? Are Governments instituted, or provided for, by God in His plans for the government of earth? Does God set up Nations and pull down Nations? Is man, by nature, a political creature, or has necessity for common safety and protection, since his corruption by the fall, *forced* him to aggregate? Or, as the Kingdom of Babel, the first kingdom noted in Scripture, was one growing out of rebellion against the decree of God to scatter or disperse; and as a stop or check was given it by the Lord, by the confounding of their language, and thus they were compelled to disperse: does this not seem to argue that God designed man should not have organic governments, but to live widespread over the earth, making no nearer approach to organic governments than the patriarchal system? Or, again: If God created and designed man to be a political creature, and necessitated aggregation, does the Bible disclose the facts? and has God instituted a government or Governments on earth? and if so, what ones? In short: Is the Bible political as well as spiritual? These are all questions that naturally suggest themselves to investigating minds. And in answer to the above, we hesitate not to say the Bible is not only political, but just as much so as it is spiritual. And as to the amount or quantum written in it, the political has largely the advantage; not that it is as important as the spiritual, but that something new and suited to all time should be recorded; each record to be known in its time by fullfilment and spiritual revealment: while the spiritual is never changing—but ever the same in all ages. What was gospel light and life for the early church is the same now, and will be forever. Hence it was not needful that a new revealment be made in every age to provide for the salvation of the soul. 'Christ and him crucified" was effectual on the Day of Pentecost; and as " there remaineth no more sacrifice for sin," it is still, and ever will be so. It was not necessary to write so much upon that subject: what was enough, God's wisdom and mercy determined, and gave it to the early church. We have it; and God is no respecter of persons: but every one that feareth God and worketh righteousness is accepted of him. In further answer to the interrogatories: We say God created and designed man to be a political creature, and necessitated aggregation; and that God has instituted a government and governments on earth, that He claims and calls his own. These facts the Bible fully discloses, as we shall see.

We state the government and governments thus: The Kingdom of Israel, under Ephraim as the first head, made up of the thirteen political Tribes, States or Governments, leaving Levi out, who had *no national existence as a Tribe*; as *individuals* they were as much political as any other *persons*. This kingdom stood about 500 years, and was, after secession, reorganized under Judah as the second head, embracing, as did the first, " all Israel." This kingdom—or rather this head—stood 73 years, and fell to pieces; ten tribes in blood, but eleven in organism, re-established the kingdom of Ephraim, with Samaria as the capital. This was not a full head; 'twas but a fraction. The other two tribes, under Judah, remained as they were—but a fraction—and these two fractions after some generations went into total captivity, Judah's fraction outliving the other about 150 years. The kingdom of Israel under Manasseh, as the 3rd and last head, under the typical dispensation, made up of thirteen Tribes or States, in answer to oft repeated promises, appears in 1776. This kingdom stood 84 years and has fallen to pieces by secession, and the first head of the kingdom of Israel, under the new or realizing dispensation under Judah, has appeared; and as she is to be realizing, she cannot pass away. The two remaining heads, Ephraim and Manasseh are yet to be found in the non-seceding States. They are to reorganize as separate heads, making the fifth and sixth heads, and then to be given to Judah, when they will become "One nation upon the mountains or governments of Israel forever." All up to this point has only been in part realizing. The of the word of the Lord .to Isral." All this strictly of *nations;* and, as such, must be largely political or governmeutal. Jeremiah 1 ch : 5 v., says that the Lord said unto him, that before he was formed or born, He (the Lord) had sanctified and ordained him a prophet *unto the nations;* and 10 v. he is set over the nations and kingdoms "to root out and to pull down and to destroy and to throw down, to *build* and to *plant.*" In verse 18th he is made "a defenced city and an iron pillar, and a brazen wall *against* the whole land, against the kings of Judah, against the princes, priests and people." Thus we might multiply passages to prove that the Prophets were largely Political Teachers; and, as such, we are bound to receive and consider their writings, and to take heed thereto, as unto "lights shining in a dark place." For in the Prophets doubtless are to be found the histories in outline, and sometimes in minute detail, of all nations and kingdoms, from their day until the curse is removed, and the time comes wherein our Saviour says, "Behold I make all things new." If such be the fact, it behooves us to remember and obey this injunction of our Saviour : "Search the scriptures;" for certainly therein is to be found our political as well as spiritual life. For while we hold, with all Christians, that the sacred scriptures disclose that full and ample provisions are made by God for our spiritual wellbeing, we claim also that the Prophets teach. and fully too, that the same beneficent Parent has made just the same provision for our social and political prosperity, being as much the author of our social, and hence our political nature, as he is of our spiritual nature ; and we affirm that the same agencies, in the main, are brought to bear in both departments of his government to effect the object desired. We are aware that this is controverted ground, and that most, if not all, biblical scholars down to Mr. Baldwin, (whom we except,) claim that all those prophecies touching Christ and his offices are *purely spiritual.* We dissent from this, and give what we believe to be the reason why those scriptures are misunderstood and an exclusively spiritual meaning given them. First, we are averse to truth and receive it reluctantly, and any doctrine readily and willingly received by us may well be suspected of error ; for the scriptures pronounce us all *liars,* and justly asserts the "truth is not in us." But perhaps the greater reason is this : Christ is *first* brought to our view as a spiritual deliverer, which is always a *personal* matter with each individual, and is in fact transcendantly the greater deliverance, and will of necessity preoccupy and absorb the mind to the exclusion of the lesser. When brought to see and feel the need of a spiritual Saviour, being exceedingly selfish, we care less for the national salvation, and hence give it little or no thought. and therefore *will not* see it. And again : spiritualities are intangible, not visible, not palpable ; they are wrapped in mystery ; we grope in darkness seeking light, and hence we *feel* the necessity of a spiritual guide. We cannot, single handed and alone. grapple with the mighty issues shut up in eternity, and are *compelled* to have a spiritual deliverer. Not altogether so in our social capacity. True, we are just as *helpless* in the one case as the other, but not being a *personal* matter we never can be made to see and feel it so sensibly ; for we will not, cannot, and should not feel the same interest in political as in spiritual concerns. In social or national affairs we have our eyes about us, and things are not so enveloped in darkness and mystery. We have our ears to hear, our hands to help ourselves; our companions, friends, relatives, whole communities and States. These, we are disposed to think, are enough. Our earthly affairs we can manage *ourselves.* Thus it is we do not see and feel the need of a political Saviour, and are not willing "to have the man Christ Jesus to reign over us." The Jews, at the coming of our Saviour, were quite differently circumstanced, and we find them acting otherwise. They having the Ceremonial Law, with its outward works, —priests. sacrifices for sin, &c.. &c.,in splendid working order.—(as we may suppose) instituted by God himself, through their great law-giver, (to which they cling to this day,) did not see and feel the need of a spiritual deliverer, being fully satisfied with what God had already given them, hence we find them unprepared and totally unwilling to receive Christ as their High Priest, and vilely rejecting him as a spiritual deliverer, yet as a king or temporal ruler the masses, unlike us, were not only willing but eager to receive him for here they felt in need. Their kingdom being overthrown by, and themselves under the rule of the Roman government, they thirsted for a political redeemer; and on ono occasion our Saviour had to flee the multitude to keep them from taking him by force and making him a king. We see that even his immediate followers could not give up the long cherished wish and expectation of a political ruler, and asked him if he would at that time restore the kingdom to Israel. True, there was a class of Jews who were *officiaries* under the Romans, and fearing that a change in rulers would remove them from position, made it the ground of accusation against Christ that "he maketh himself a king," and hence "speaketh against Cæsar." Pilate asked them if he should crucify their king, and they replied "We have no king but Cæsar," showing clearly that they understood him to be a king as well as a priest. Christ himself in answer to Pilate's question "Art thou a king then?" replied "Thou sayest that I am a king. To this end was I born, and for this cause came I into the world." This, we think, is sufficient to settle his kingship. But some will doubtless say his kingdom was spiritual ; and, in support of that position, will repeat his reply to Pilate, "My kingdom is not of this world." True, he so said, meaning evidently the Roman world, over which they accused him of desiring to reign, to the subversion of Cæsar; which, in the above, he disclaims, and fully satisfies Pilate that he is guiltless of the charge.

We are assured by the most learned biblical scholars that the word *world* in the Hebrew has upward of twenty significations, *only one* of which mean the earth or globe on which we live, and that it is often used as Christ here uses it in reference to the Roman polity ; this, however, no scholar will deny. Why then did he not assume the reigns of government and rule his people nationally, and deliver them from Roman bondage? He does not tell us why; while it is very evident that the more important part of his mission claimed his first attention viz. : the spiritual redemption of the world : and if he had then thought proper to set up a political reign, it would not have been over the little Jewish and Israelitish tribes, but over the whole earth ; for, if a king in any sense, "He is King of Kings and Lord of Lords."

But, as above, the more important part of his mission claimed his first attention, to fulfil which he must be offered up as a sacrifice for sin, must die to redeem the world, and must consequently defer the setting up *fully* of the other department of his government until some future time in his wisdom set. But if some will still cling to long received and cherished tenets or doctrines, and contend that his kingdom is not of this world, they would unhinge the whole christian system, and prove that there is no such thing as a *spiritual kingdom* in this world; and thereby prove too much for their own cause. The fact is, Christ was not arraigned before Pilate for spiritual heresies, but solely for political offences, as is clearly shown by every question the governor asked him, as recorded by the four Evangelists. The first question, as given by each of them, is, "Art thou the king of the Jews?" to which, in every case, he answers affirmatively; but at the same time to the satisfaction of Pilate, who represents Cæsar in the case. So we find in this *political* trial he is accused of the *political* sin against the Roman government, of claiming to be a king within its jurisdiction; add he admits and claims indeed that he is a political king, for he was on a political trial, before a political court, that had no jurisdiction in spiritual matters. So far he does not deny the charge, yet he is held guiltless, because his kingdom does not infringe upon Cæsar's. It would have been irrelevant, when asked of political matters, to have answered of spiritual ones, upon which he was not questioned. His questions were political, and his answers must of necessity have been so too—hence the answer "My kingdom is not of this world" was not one of reference to his priestly office or spiritual matters, for that was not brought in question ; but he was questioned politically, and only politically. Could his answers be construed otherwise? And if not, he truly said "For this cause came I into the world,"—not saying, however, that that was the alone cause. In short, the All wise and merciful God, determining to provide a full redemption for His fallen world, sets about it in wisdom, and first brings to light the spiritual redemption as the most important and *absolutely necessary* to effect political salvation, for without the first we could never attain unto the second. We affirm then, on good authority, that Christ is a "Prophet, Priest and King." First, a prophet means in one of its nearest and most legitimate senses, a teacher, as well as a foreteller ; and we say he does teach in the two several departments of his government. All are ready to admit, as Prophet, he has ever taught, and largely too, in the spiritual department of his government. First, by himself, while on earth; secondly, by his spirit; thirdly, by the written word, called the sword of the spirit; fourthly, by a called and accredited living ministry ; fifthly, by providences in almost endless variety ; "line upon line, and precept upon precept ; here a little and there a little." In inaugurating and setting up fully his priestly department, it was necessary that he should become himself a sacrifice for sin, which he did on Mount Calvary. crying, in his last moment, "It is finished !" by which we understand the spiritual redemption of the world ; was finished, so far as the great High Priest's *offering* was concerned, "For there remaineth no more sacrifice for sin." This kingdom being set up, and the above enumerated agencies brought to bear on the hearts and consciences of the people, we read that on the day of Pentecost three thousand rushed into the kingdom ; and they still continue to come, to the present day., Here we have no force or martial array brought to view : all is invitation, persuasion, wooing and entreating ; "Come, for all things are now ready," by which is meant all has been done that will be done without our agency. We must now act; no force is to be used; this kingdom deals with free agents ; and, mark you, with *individuals.* "Ho! every *one* that thirsteth, come," and "*Him* that will let him come." He must reign here in the hearts and affections of his subjects *individually.* Now, to become a subject of this kingdom, the cardinal and absolute requirements are belief in Christ as its head; and, believing, to heartily repent of and turn away from sin, and receive him as a Saviour. When we come to take a view of his political kingdom, we find it very different. True, there is much persuasion, much leading, much enlargement ; here, also; much teaching in his prophetic capacity; much by his holy spirit's influence on the great political heart; and much, very much, in his written word; and by the human agencies that he has called and qualified, from Adam to Noah, to Abraham, to Moses and Joshua, to David, and from him until the present time of an inviting and persuasive character—thus evincing the great and compassionate regard that our God has for his intelligent, yet dependent creatures— showing that he would ever lead and never force, if we would but be led. But we, refusing to be guided and influenced by the aforesaid appliances, by "Hardening our hearts and stiffening our necks," are in danger of being "suddenly destroyed, and that without remedy ;" for at this point a great deal of kingly force is brought to view, (never visible in his *priestly* department,) which marks his kingly office so distinctly, and separates it so widely from his priestly office, that it does seem the most casual observer need not doubt as to the *identity* of the *two* departments of his government on this sin cursed earth of ours. We know and admit there is much in the prophets, touching the prosperity of Christ's kingdom that will in truth apply to both departments, and so intended by inspiration, for the two are so closely allied, (*not joined*) that the one cannot truthfully be said to be very prosperous while the other is the reverse. One may be appropriately styled the handmaid of the other. We suppose that no one in this enlightened age will deny that, as the Church has soared or sunk, so has the State.

That we must be pure *individually,* before we can be collectively, is as self-evident a fact as that it requires salt springs to make, when collected, a salt river or lake. Hence, it becomes every individual, who would be a true patriot under God, to 'seek first the kingdom of heaven ;" that is, seek to be spiritually inducted into the first department of his government, to first become a Christian, or follower of Christ, the great High Priest ; and the promise is "That all these things shall be added unto you ;" that is, all needed temporal blessings. Again : there are prophecies so exclusively spiritual, that they can hardly be said to contain anything political, while there are others altogether political, and very many that are not solvable at this day, but will be in their time, as many are now, that were not formerly, their time not having come.

From the foregoing, it will be seen how very important it is that the mind's eye be kept on *both departments* of God's government, in order to read, understandingly, the Prophets ; and we include all that is prophetic from Genesis to Revelation.

CHAPTER THIRD.

AS we have asserted, and do assert, that the *three* Israelitish Kingdoms were of God, it will be expected of us to show the facts fully ; and in doing so, we will go further back than the governments themselves further back than the fathers and patriarchs to whom they were promised. We will even venture to go back to God himself, the fountain and source of all true governments ; and if so, they must be like him, or "God like," for "like begets like." So it is needful in determining the likeness of the governments, to first determine the likeness of God, their author ; to do which we will go to His own record of Himself, as we find it in the Bible, and in His intellectual and physical creations.

God is said to be *one*, and at the same time to be *three*, thus making *four* ; and his trinity is repeated, making his number of perfection seven. How is this to be explained? how to be understood? It is to be understood thus : God in *essence* is *essentially* and *absolutely one*, *invisible*, *unoriginated* and *eternal*. In *attributes*, *character*, or *quality* he is *three*, viz.: Omnipotent, Omniscient and Omnipresent, thus making *four* ; but these three attributes being further made known, or in mercy brought down to the better comprehension of his creature man, by repeating his trinity, appear as Father, Son and Holy Spirit. This double form of *threes* go to make up the *one* God who is the *seventh* and last form of the Godhead.— Less than this he could not have and be God ; more than this is an impossibility. We could not conceive of a God without the *three* first named, nor have we the power to conceive of more than is embraced in the *three* as repeated. They do embrace *all*, and more than *all* is a positive impossibility. So then God in *essence* is *essentially* and *absolutely one*, and at the same time essentially *three* in *quality*, as he is absolutely *three* in *persons*—thus making, as before stated, *seven*. The Father is not God independent of the Son and Spirit, neither is the Son apart from the Father and spirit, nor the spirit separate from Father and Son. So it is plain that God is not a union *upon any one* of the *three*, but is a union *of* the three, and hence necessarily makes a *fourth* form in the Godhead, which indeed is *the* God of the three persons above, and different from them in their individuality, and must have his individual number as they each have. Thus : The Father is one, the Son is one, the spirit is one, and a union of them all is one, which is the God, and the fourth in number. The same is true of the attributes : Omnipotence is one, Omniscience is one, and Omnipresent is one, and a union of them is one, and the other, God, is one that the union of the personal trinity made. The God is the same God, and number four in both of the trinities, and not a *different* number four, which some might mistake at first thought and add up eight, when really there are but *seven*, which is God's number of *perfection*. Again : This *one* God is made up of numerous traits, features or lineaments, viz : goodness, mercy, truth, love, patience, justice, forbearance, forgiveness, gentleness, fatherly care, &c., &c. God is not make all these, but they make up the God. To obtain a true or correct idea of God we must do so through the mediums he has furnished us, by the aid and assistance of his Holy Spirit, for of ourselves we can do nothing. The God leads that come within the range of human comprehension, we take up, step by step, until we arrive at God. We can sooner comprehend the import of goodness, mercy, love, &c., than we can the abstract idea of God. We must first take hold of the idea of goodness, mercy, love, &c., we very naturally turn to the source from whence they flow ; we begin to arrive. We conclude that to be good to us, the source of the goodness must be present with us, and this presence necessitates Omnipresence ; and this quality leads us to the Omnipotence, and these two still further necessitate

Omniscience; and once again these three qualities joined or united, necessitate a God; and so on through the whole round of traits of character, we are necessitated up to the grand idea of the self-existent Eternal.

The various lineaments are not God, but make Him known to us. They are mediums through which we are taught by the Spirit to apprehend him.

We have remarked that God's number of perfection is seven; that is, in *assending* up to God we fill up the number seven. Thus: The Holy Spirit is one, the Son is one, the Father is one, Omnipresence is one, Omniscience is one, Omnipotence is one, and all taken together is one, and only one, yet in number, seven. Now, the foregoing being considered, might we not, nay! are we not *forced* to the conclusion that the visible creations of this three one God, twice told, should partake of this three one form, twice told. That "like begets like" is a truism, a Bible taught fact not to be doubted, and hence we are warranted in expecting the child or creature to resemble the parent or creator, in visible outlines at least, if not in every lineament or feature. First then, of the visible creation—though not first in order of time—we will take up the creature man; and we are at once informed that "in the image," and again "in the likeness" of God was he created. How? we would ask; in what sense is man "in the image of God?" Is he Omnipotent, &c? No! he is not, or he would be God. Some will, doubtless, say reference is here had to God's holiness or purity, as the "image." We say not; for if he was as pure, holy, or perfect, as God was and is, he never would have fallen by temptation, as he certainly did, for "God cannot be tempted." In what sense, then, is man "like God?" We answer, he is like God in that he conforms to the Triune God : first, in his personal body, soul and spirit. The Bible says he is so formed or possessed of the three, and we are not disposed to dissent from such high authority, or to further argue the point, as this will settle it at once. And secondly, as we found God was repeated in His trinity, we also find man repeated in his trinity. In physical man there are *three* essential fountains of life, and *only three*, neither of which could exist independent of the other two, viz : the brain, or nervous system ; the heart, or circulating system ; and the lungs, or breathing system. Here you will see again the three as before noted, of body, soul, and spirit, but the last three constitute but one, and the very same man that was expressed by the first trinity of body, soul and spirit. The body is one, the soul is one, the spirit is one, the brain is one, the heart is one, the lung is one, and all taken together are one, and only one, yet in number seven. These are all essentials of life. You may dismember and mutilate man as you will, so as the brain, blood and breathing systems are not cut off, and he continues to live, and is, to all intents and purposes, a man. Many are born imperfect as to both bodily and mental structure, yet are "living souls," and hence *are men*. If any doubt the correctness of our conclusions as to the "image" of God in which man was created, we need give but one scripture, or "thus saith the Lord" to settle the point, as we think. Genesis 1 ch: 26 v God said "Let *us* make man in *our* image, after *our* likeness." Here it is unequivocally asserted that the God who spoke above was a *plural* God. Let *us* make "in *our*"—"after our." Thus the plural Godhead in its full plurality of Omnipotence, Omniscience, Omnipresence, Father, Son and Holy Spirit sits in the council of Heaven and determines and says "let *us* make," and then did make man in the "image of God." Less than the whole council could not have said "let us make," and then have made man in the image agreed upon. No person or attribute could by possibility be left out. All spake and all acted ; six Gods sat in council and spake, and the very same six responsive acted, and a corresponding creature is the natural result ; so man must of necessity be like *all* of them in some sense, and as he cannot be by possibility like them in attributes of Omnipotence, Omniscience and Omnipresence ; nor yet like them in the persons of Father, Son and Holy Spirit, it follows inevitably that he is like them in numbers. He can and does have their number seven, the identical "image" intended by inspiration. It is not possible that God could be "imaged" in man in any other mode than that of numbers. Spiritual existence cannot be imaged, cannot be portrayed in tangible form ; no delineation is possible to our powers of apprehension. The only delineated image of God is found in his numbers, and his image of numbers is that in which man was created. And numbers themselves, in the abstract, are as intangible as a spirit, but they have their representatives in visible figures, which visible is seized upon to portray or set forth the invisible. The "image" above was evidently one of *plurality*, and not of *nature, state* or *condition*. Should it be said animals conform to one of the triune forms of God, and are also "God like," viz: brain, heart and lungs, we agree, and claim in support of our position that all nature, animate and inanimate, must in a greater or less degree be 'Godlike," for "like begets like" throughout the universe. What further is taught us in the Bible of this triune man? That being tempted, he fell by transgression, and became so corrupt that God repented him that he had made man, and by a flood swept him from the earth, leaving only four males. Noah, who represents God both in *person* and *power*, divides himself so to speak, into three bloodheads, or a trinity of bloods, represented by his three sons Shem, Ham and Japheth, and being the heir of the world, he divides it into a trinity of territory, assigning to each bloodhead his inheritance. Here we have a trinity of persons yet only *one* in their father representing a trinity of blood, who in Noah was only one blood, and also a trinity of territory, making but one earth. This is a trinity of trinities. Following one of these bloodheads, represented by Shem, the eldest of Noah's three sons, to whom national rule was first promised—he was first to sway the national sceptre—we soon find in it a trinity of national fathers in Abraham, Isaac and Jacob ; and in Jacob's house the trinity of national fathers is repeated and represented by Ephraim, Judah and Manasseh. Thus, as in repeating of the triune God, we found seven; so also we do here of the national fathers, viz.: Manasseh was one, Judah was one, Ephraim was one. Jacob was one. Isaac was one, Abraham was one, and all taken together is but the one promised nationality to Shem. who is the seventh, being the first in promise and is to be the last in realization. We always trace upward to the head: return to the place of beginning. The trinity of blood we do not find repeated ; it is not necessary to do so to express fullness or completion. The Godhead was fully expressed by the first trinity of the attributes ; no more was embraced in the second Trinity than was found in the first. The result in both was God. Yet as we say it was in mercy repeated, for the better comprehension of man, so any trinity within itself is complete. and the result in all cases is a fourth in number, and not either one of the trinity numbers. Japheth was one. Ham was one, Shem was one. and all taken together constitute or represent Noah as one blood, which indeed he was, but yet three in his sons. The Bible is silent as to any effort, so to speak, on the part of God to institute organic governments on earth before the flood. The patriarchal system seems to have been the nearest approach to it. But after the flood God determines upon a reorganization in general. in which reorganization the political or national comes in and begins at the beginning. Shem was to sway the national sceptre first, as God's representative on earth, and was to be succeeded by his brother Japheth, who will sway it until "he comes whose it is." The patriarchal system prevails after the flood for a considerable time. but even it makes an advance as the days of Abraham, a regal descendant of Shem, with whom God makes a covenant *national;* renews it in the same words to his son and regal heir, Isaac ; again renews it in like words to Isaac's regal son and heir, Jacob, saying a "nation and a company of nations" was to be of them. The three national fathers above, not realizing this repeated promise in themselves, Jacob. the last one of the three, transfers the promise to his three regal sons Ephraim, Judah and Manasseh. How remarkable! Here we have a trinity of promises, yet the promise itself is but one. It is the identical promise to all three—a nationality to be made up of nationalities—first promised to Abraham, then to Isaac. and then to Jacob. The promise was not to Abraham of one certain nationality, and to Isaac and Jacob of two other nationalities, but to all three of the same one. As the first, or father, did not realize the fulfillment of the promise, it descended to his son Isaac, and he, failing to realize it, it is transferred to Jacob, who in turn transfers it to his sons as a trinity. each of which was to receive it by turns and pass it to the next. So we have *two* trinities of promises, or rather the same promise made to two trinities, again making the number six. Neither one of the numbers running up to six was the *very thing* promised, but a full realization is to be found in a union of both the trinities, making the seventh number and last form, or head of, the nationality promised. The three first fathers never did receive the semblance of a kingdom, except Jacob may be said to have done so in his twelve sons and their families, who shadowed forth visibly the coming nation, made up of a "company of nations." They were one family, made up of a number of families. This would indicate that the three first heads of the promised nation would be typical or non-realizing, and that the third head, or last of the three, whom Jacob represents, was to be *more realizing* than the two preceding ones. We will have occasion to notice this point again, when we come to speak of realization elsewhere. We will now turn to the promises referred to, and trace up the nationality, under its several heads. of the first or non-realizing trinity ; remarking, however, upon trinities that *nothing exists without its trinity*, not even inanimate substances. 'Tis impossible to conceive of anything or give expression of it, without making use of a trinity in some mode. For instance, take a book, block of wood, stone, or even the most attenuated web of the spider, or sheet of paper, or anything, no matter how irregular in form, and it must and does have *length, breadth* and *thickness*. Not because the books say so, but the books say so, because they are positively inherent qualities of all substances. You may say the body is round or square, and it will give no idea of its size or dimensions ; for though it may be round or square, or of any other form, it must of necessity have length, breadth and thickness *expressed* before you can conceive of or estimate it.

CHAPTER FOURTH.

THE KINGDOM OF ISRAEL UNDER EPHRAIM, OR ITS FIRST HEAD.

IN Genesis 12 ch: 2 v. God says to Abraham "I will make of thee a great nation." Gen. 17 ch: 4 v. "Thou shalt be a father of many nations." Gen. 18 ch: 18 v. "Abraham shall surely become a great and mighty nation." Here, at the very outset, we have a nation in its *oneness* and also in *severalty* or plural form, of which we shall have occasion to speak more largely hereafter ; so please bear in mind this : "E pluribus unum." Again, Gen. 22 ch: 17 v. it was promised to Abraham that his seed "should be as the stars of heaven, and as the sand on the sea shore, and that they should possess the gates of their enemies." Here is aggressiveness, and must be national, not individuals. "And in thy seed shall all nations of the earth be blessed." These promises are renewed Gen 16 ch: 3 and 4 v. to Isaac. In Gen. 25 ch: 23 v. it is said to Rebecca "two nations are in thy womb," which were Jacob and Esau, her then unborn sons, typifying or representing two great nationalities that were to arise from them, which promise had its fulfillment in the kingdoms of Israel and Edom. This, we suppose, no one will question. Isaac blessing Jacob says, Gen. 27 ch: 29 v., "Let people serve thee, and *nations* bow down to thee," as much as to say people shall serve thee, and nations shall bow down to thee, for it was spoken prophetically, and therefore must find fulfillment, or the truth of scripture must fail. And as nations are made to bow down, it must be to a nation or nations that they bow, for to Jacob as an individual they did not bow down ; he was only the representative of the "nation or nations" to whom obedience is commanded. Again it is said to Jacob, "A nation and a company of nations shall be of thee, and kings shall come out of thy loins"— the same promise precisely that was made to his grandfather Abraham and renewed to Isaac, as quoted above; showing the *one* of *many* and the *many* in *one*, so often seen emblazoned on our old national standard, coin, &c. Once more : of Ephraim it is said, Gen. 48 ch : 19 v., "His seed shall become a multitude of nations." And Balaam, in blessing the house of

13

Jacob says, in Num 24 ch: 8 v., "God brought him forth out of Egypt, he hath as it were the strength of an unicorn: he shall eat up the nations his enemies, and shall break their bones, and pierce them through with his arrows." All this can be said of nations only, and therefore is clearly political, and proves to a demonstration that the allwise and merciful God does concern himself in the political affairs of earth, as well as the spiritual, and that he "pulleth down one nation and setteth up another as seemeth good to him." It further proves that he not only takes cognizance of the national or political affairs of earth, but that he has (as we shall be able to show,) had "a nation and a company of nations" that he in an especial sense called his own, from Abraham, in whom they were in embryo, until the consummation of all things earthly. We might go on multiplying passages as above, but our limits forbid, and the readers patience might tire; besides, we deem the foregoing sufficient, for, as said to one of old, "They have Moses and the prophets: if they will not hear them, they would not believe though one should arise from the dead."

We will now set out in search of the "nation and company of nations" promised; and in this we shall be a *pioneer*, for so far as we know no one has undertaken to tread the path we now propose to travel. The nation as *one* we need not discuss, as all will readily admit that the descendants of Abraham (called Hebrews,) delivered from the bondage of Egypt by the Lord, through his servants Moses and Aaron, and finally by Joshua brought to, and put in possession of, the land of Canaan in an organized, national form, is the identical nation above named as *one*. Now, that *same* nation in its plural heads of three, we seek for, and shall not seek in vain. We shall notice what is said in the promises concerning them, for whatever is promised must be realized or fulfilled; and whatever is foretold of them, is equivalent to a promise. The "company of nations" above in *one* of its forms, for it has seven, begins to take form and appear first in the 48 ch. of Gen., where Jacob blesses his sons, takes Ephraim and Manasseh, the two sons of Joseph, from their father and adopts them as his own sons, saying "as Reuben and Simeon, they shall be mine." He then proceeds to pronounce a national blessing, or promise, upon these two sons, placing his right hand upon the head of Ephraim, and his left upon the head of Manasseh, saying, in the 16th verse: "The Angel which redeemed me from all evil, bless the lads; and let my name" (Israel, which signifies to prevail,) "be named on them, and the name of my fathers Abraham and Isaac; and let them grow into a multitude in the midst of the earth;" and in the 19th verse said they both should become a people, and not only so, but "a great people;" but that Ephraim should be greater than his brother Manasseh, and "should become a multitude of nations." In the 20th verse the Israelitish nation should bless "saying, God made thee as Ephraim and as Menasseh: and he set Ephraim before Manasseh." And herein consisted his greatness, as contrasted with his brother Manasseh. He was simply to have national rule or dominion first, for they were both to be precisely the same thing, "a great people," but Ephraim before Manasseh. Manasseh was as certain to follow as Ephraim was to lead. And if Ephraim's blessing conferred national rule or leadship upon *him*, equally so does Manasseh's, for their blessing was *one* as to what was conferred, and *two* as to *time*. As some will doubtless question whether the blessing carried with it national headship, we will give some pointed scriptures that will establish the fact beyond a doubt. 1st Chronicles, 5 ch: 1 v. says that Reuben's birthright was taken from him and "was given unto the sons of Joseph the son of Israel." Now, why is Joseph here called, as also in other scriptures, "the son of Israel," the prevailer with God and man, if it did not signify his superiority over his brethren? with the exception of Judah, who in the 2nd verse is said to have "prevailed above his brethren, and of him came the chief ruler; but the birthright was Joseph's." The fact is, Joseph being the son by preeminence above his brethren, of his prevailing father Israel, he became the head and inherited the right to rule or prevail. This being made still stronger, if possible, by saying his was the birthright, which always gave and carried with it the dominion over the balance of the household and a double inheritance, except as in the case of Reuben and Esau, it was specifically disposed of. This

14

would seem to be sufficient, but as we travel an untrodden road, (to us at least,) we will add further marks from the same unquestioned authority to fortify the position wo have taken, and will cite Jacob's blessing of Joseph. (which always descends by heirship to the sons.) Gen. 49 ch: 22 v., Joseph is called "a fruitful bough by a well; whose branches run over a wall." What wall is here spoken of in the past tense, yet evidently in the future, but his national wall or boundary that he was to break over? showing at once the aggressive character of the nation he represented. 25th verse he was to be sustained nationally by the God of heaven, "with the blessings of heaven above, blessings of the deep, blessings of ●
the breast, and of the womb." 26th v., "The blessings of thy father have prevailed above the blessings of my progenitors unto the utmost bound of the everlasting hills: they" (the foregoing blessing,) "shall be on the head of Joseph, and on the crown of the head of him that was separate from his brethren." Once more: Deut. 33 ch: 13 v., "Blessed of the Lord his land, for the precious things of heaven, for the dew, and for the deep that coucheth beneath, and for the precious fruits brought forth by the sun, and for the precious things put forth by the moon, and for the chief things of the ancient mountains, and for the precious things of the lasting hills, and for the precious things of the earth and fulness thereof, and for the good will of him that dwelt in the bush: let the blessing" (above) "come upon the head of Joseph, and upon the top of the head of him that was separated from his brethren. His glory the firstling of his bullock, and his horns the horns of unicorns: with them" (the horns,) "he shall push the people together to the ends of the earth: and they" (the horns,) " are the ten thousand of Ephraim, and they are the thousands of Manasseh." This is surely sufficient, for the present at least, and is national in its character throughout; and in no future sense does it apply to the *person* Joseph, nor yet to his two sons, who heir all conferred on the father. Joseph's future was at no time more glorious or exalted than when the above was spoken of him, and hence cannot apply to him personally, but strictly of his future headship and rule over the Israelitish nation in its *oneness*, by one of his sons at a time in his tribal capacity; first, Ephraim, as it is said "he set Ephraim before Manasseh." It follows, then, if Ephraim leads, Menasseh must come after him in the same capacity of ruler; and it further follows that if they reign over the same nation, they must do so at different periods of time. it being impossible for both to reign at once over a united people, or over this one nation promised to each of the three fathers, as one, and this one nation under each head, was to be made up of "a company of nations." So they must rule at different times.

Having said what we deem sufficient as to the *promises of nationality* to Abraham, who received it not, and as his successors Isaac, Jacob, Judah, Ephraim and Manasseh did not live to see the end of the Egyptian bondage, we will now go beyond in the history of that interesting people, and find a fulfillment of the promises; in which we shall certainly be anticipated by all Bible readers, as to the first single form of the nation. We will start at the point of time that the Hebrews (about 3,000,000 in number, 600,000 of whom were able to draw the sword, under the leadership of Moses,) left the land of bondage for the land of promise, and will follow them rapidly through their forty years wandering in the wilderness, into the land of promise, with Joshua, an Ephraimite, at their head as Captain General and leader of their hosts in battle. We find that under this Ephraimitish leader this wandering, migratory Hebrew people rapidly subdued, drove out and put to the sword the nations that were in possession of the land, and organized in their stead, the first *theocratic*, *states-rights*, *confederate*, *republican* government on earth, with Joshua as the first President, Judge, or Chief Executive. Thus *began* to be fulfilled the oft-repeated promises to the patriarchal fathers of nationality; and this organic structure, under the Ephraimitish head in its *oneness*, and under the thirteen *tribal* heads in its *severalty* or *plural* form of sovereign States, remained intact for about five centuries; but finally under Samuel, the last Judge or President, the people, by the permission of God, added to their republic *royalty*, with Saul, a Benjaminite, chosen by God, and anointed by Samuel, as their first king. But this addition did not affect the theocratic, confederate, states-right form of government; it only gave their political head the title and prerogatives of a king. This nationality under all of its heads is always called in scripture "Israel." Its capital under the first head was Shiloh, in the tribe of Ephraim, and the people were also called Hebrews, and descended in a direct line from Shem, the eldest of Noah's three sons; and the government, as before stated, was one of many, or many in one, or perhaps more properly it was a singular made up of plurals, and answers to the promise "a nation and a company of nations" that was to be fulfilled to Ephraim; and so it was, as above noted. Here, for the present, we will drop the kingdom or government of Ephraim, and go in search of "Judah's Kingdom," for national headship was also promised him, as well as Ephraim and Manasseh; and as Manasseh is found later in history and prophetic fulfillment than Judah, we will take up Judah first and Manasseh last of the three, for be it known, once for all, that we claim that the Bible teaches that there was to arise three typical. E pluribus unum, governments or nationalities; one under Ephraim, one under Judah, and one under Manasseh, promised first to Abraham, Isaac, and Jacob.

CHAPTER FIFTH.

THE KINGDOM OF ISRAEL UNDER DAVID OR JUDAH.

IN accordance with our plan, we now take up the nationality of Judah, as we find it in scripture promises, commonly called *blessings*. Jacob, in the 19th ch: 1 v. of Gen., "called unto his sons, and said, Gather yourselves together, that I may tell you that which shall befall you in the last days." Of course he did not mean what was to befall his twelve *individual* sons, for that of which he was about to speak, was to *befall* them "*in the latter days*," which to say the least, was a remote or distant time, and was consequently spoken of them in their descendants and in a national sense. In the 8th verse Jacob says: "Judah, thou art he whom thy brethren shall praise; thy hand shall be in the neck of thine enemies; thy father's children shall bow down before thee. Judah is a lion's whelp: from the prey, my son, thou art gone up: he stooped down, he couched as a lion, and as an old lion; who shall rouse him up? The sceptre shall not depart," &c. This is all national, and in the far future; for his literal brethren never did bow to him, nor have we any evidence that he ever had his hand in the neck of his enemies, or that any preeminence whatever was his: and in fact he bowed down, together with his brethren, to Joseph their brother, when they went down into Egypt. It is all prophetic of the future of Jacob's sons nationally. They were all (Levi excepted) promised nationality, but to Judah and Joseph alone was promised national headship or dominion over the other tribes or states. 1st Chron., 5 ch: 2 v. "For Judah prevailed above his brethren, and of him came the chief ruler." This, with many other passages, is spoken in the past tense, but is of necessity future. In Psalm 60th: 7 v. is said "Gilead is mine, and Manasseh is mine; Ephraim also is the strength of mine head; Judah is my lawgiver;" and if a lawgiver, he must have been so nationally, for at this writing Judah had been dead many generations. In the 78th Psalm, 67th verse: "Moreover he" (the Lord) "refused the tabernacle of Joseph, and chose not the tribe of Ephraim: but chose the tribe of Judah, the mount Zion which he loved. And he built his sanctuary like high palaces, like the earth which he hath established for ever." This passage proves that Ephraim's reign has an end, but Judah's, under David, shall be endless as the earth; and this proves that Judah and mount Zion are one and the same "Judah the mount Zion which he loved."

In the 89th Psalm. 3 v., is said, "I have made a covenant with my chosen, I have sworn unto David my servant, thy seed will I establish forever, and build up thy throne to all generations." Now, all that is said of David applies to Judah, for . he was Judah's head; and applies also to mount Zion, for it was "Judah" the mount Zion which he loved." Again, in the 19th verse, some Psalm of David, it is said, "I have laid help upon one that is mighty; I have exalted one chosen out of the people. I have found David my servant; with my holy oil have I anointed him." . . . . . "I will beat down his foes before his face, and plague them that hate him, and in my name shall his horn be exalted. I will set his hand also in the sea, and his right hand in the rivers. He shall cry unto me" (saying) "Thou art my father, my God, and the rock of my salvation. Also I will make him my firstborn, higher than the kings of the earth. My mercy will I keep for him for evermore, and my covenant shall stand fast with him. His seed also will I make to endure for ever, and his throne as the days of heaven. My covenant will I not break, nor alter the thing that is gone out of my lips. — Once have I sworn by my holiness that I will not lie unto David. His seed shall endure forever, and his throne as the sun before me." We have here a lengthy quotation from the Psalms, penned or spoken during the reign of David or his successors, and must have a future application, yet every word of it is in *refer ence* to the Israelitish, or in other words, David's kingdom, and is strictly political. And as the then existing kingdom of David passed away eighteen hundred years ago, the above promises of perpetuity cannot be applied to it, but to its *antitype*, which was to arise in the far distant future, called often "latter day or days." But we are digressing somewhat from our present purpose, which is to show that nationality was promised to Judah, as well as to Ephraim and Manasseh; still, we may claim the last quotations as collateral supports to the former, as they go to prove the fact that there did arise such a kingdom as "Judah" or David's; and hence the former quotations, and our conclusions. are proven by the latter. We presume it will not be questioned that there was then such a kingdom as Judah's, including all Israel, as well as Ephraim's did. But that they were separate may, doubtless will, be questioned. As we have shown, or called attention to, the rise of the kingdom of Ephraim, and traced it in haste to its change into a royalty under Saul, its first king, we will now call attention to the rise of the kingdom of Judah over Israel, noting carefully its origin. In the 16 ch : 1 v. of 1st Samuel God says to Samuel the prophet : "I have rejected Saul from reigning over Israel: fill thine horn with oil, and go, I will send thee to Jesse the Beth-lehemite : for I have provided me a king among his sons. . . Then Samuel took the horn of oil, and anointed him (David) in the midst of his brethren: and the Spirit of the Lord came upon David from that day forward. . . . . But the Spirit of the Lord departed from Saul." Here, in plain terms, Saul, the first king of Israel, is rejected by God who chose him, and David, of the Jewish tribe, elected, chosen, and anointed in his stead by the same authority, but not yet crowned and formally inducted into his office. Saul, his predecessor, continues to exercise the functions of king for a considerable period of time. In the mean time, David grows popular with the people. Saul's jealousy of the embryo king appears : he bitterly persecutes, and uses every possible means to have him slain. David flees from stronghold to stronghold with his faithful and increasing little band, hard pressed by his inveterate enemy. Saul, becoming stressed by the Philistines, commandeth the woman of Endor to cause Samuel, who is now dead, to arise for his council. Samuel comes. 28 ch: 16 v., and says "Wherefore then dost thou ask of me, seeing the Lord is departed from thee, and is become thine enemy? . . . . for the Lord hath rent the kingdom out of thine hand, and given it to thy neighbor, even to David." Very soon after this is spoken, Saul falls in battle, on Mount Gilboa. David immediately enquires of the Lord whether he should go up into any of the cities of Judah; and the Lord answers "Go up to Hebron." . . . . So David went up thither. . . . . And the men of Judah came and there they anointed David king over the house of Judah." Abner, Saul's General-in-chief, about this time took Saul's son, "and made him king over all Israel," "and he reigned two years;" while David reigned over Judah in Hebron

—ven years and six months. Saul's son being in the meantime, wickedly slain "Then came all the tribes of Israel" (in their tribal capacity,) "to David unto Hebron" . . . . "and they anointed David king of Israel." "David was thirty years old when he began to reign, and he reigned forty years. In Hebron he reigned over Judah seven years and six months: and in Jerusalem he reigned thirty and three years over all Israel and Judah." Thus is given, by inspiration, the origin and rise of the kingdom of David, conferring national headship upon Judah over all Israel, for over Israel was he first anointed by the Lord in his youth, and when thirty years old anointed king over Judah; and here commenced it incipiency hereafter over "all Israel," which culminated seven years and six months thereafter. His son Solomon succeeded him, and reigned forty years over all Israel ; but on the succession of Solomon's son Rehoboam to the throne of David, ten of the tribes of Israel broke off, under the leadership of Jeroboam ; leaving (as God had before said to Solomon,) but one tribe with the house of Judah, and that tribe was Benjamin. Thus Judah's headship, over all Israel, lasted just seventy-three years : and the kingdom of Israel, under the leadership of Jeroboam, the Ephraimite, was reestablished, with Samaria as the capital, the first capital having been at Shiloh. From this time forward we find the kingdoms of Judah and Israel running parallel, with their kings cotemporary ; at times waring, and again at peace ; now prospering under a good king, or toppling to ruin under a corrupt leader : suffering divers partial captivities, until finally the kingdom of Israel, under Ephraim, went into total national captivity, under Shalmaneser—and have not, nor ever will return, under Hebrew rulers. Yet the oft repeated promise is that Israel shall return. (See 16 ch. of Ezekiel.) For this, we shall seek at the proper time and place. We are not yet done with David's kingdom in its typal reign, (for it was typical.) We follow it through varying fortunes, for about a century and a half, and find it, at the coming of Shiloh, the promised Messiah, a Roman province, a subjugated people, possessing no national head, but retaining its tribal distinction; for this had been promised by Jacob in his blessing of Judah. He was to remain intact as a tribe "until Shiloh come;" soon after which event Judah, like Ephraim, passes into endless captivity, so far as the Hebrew headship is concerned. Numerous promises, like as unto Ephraim, are dispersed through the Bible of a "latter day" return to him also ; showing, as in the case of Ephraim, that his reign had been *typical*, and not *realizing*, only in part. For this we shall also seek at the proper time and place. Our next business will be to search for the third typical head of the kingdom of Israel. which is to be fulfilled to Manasseh ; for the promises to him are as clear as they are to his two predecessors: and if the two foregoing were types, his must, of necessity, be so too, for they were brethren nationally ; or, as in the 16th ch. of Ezekiel, " Sisters."

CHAPTER SIXTH.

crate, republican royalty, or of whatever form or complexion—so were the others.
From this conclusion there is no escape. We do not say that in all their lineaments and features brothers and sisters *shall* be alike, but the general resemblance, or family marks, should be found. We hesitate not to assert, as before,
that the first organic form of the Hebrew nation was a *theocratic, confederate, states
right Republic*, under Ephraim, to which royalty, in the end, was added: and under
its second organic form royalty remained, leaving it still, however, a republic : for
the people resisted successfully the decree of death by Saul, the first king,
—claiming the right to reverse his judgment—and did so. Now, as Ephraim and
Manasseh were not, in the strict sense of the word, "brothers" of Judah—for they
were, in fact, his nephews—we may reasonably conclude there was a more strik-
ing resemblance existing between *them* than between them and him; and in like
manner between their two governments more corresponding marks than between
their governments and his. Such we find to be the case. Let us see. The first
Israel was made up of twelve sovereign, independent states, one of whom (Manasseh) was divided in settlement—thus making thirteen—leaving out Levi, who
had no landed estate, no nationality. In short, his was the priesthood. Mr.
Baldwin makes up the thirteen by including him. This was improper, as it is
said he shall have no inheritance but the priesthood, hence no nationality. We
are seeking after nations, and shall pass him by.

Mr. Baldwin, in his incomparable work, "Armageddon," has done for us
what we never could have hoped to have accomplished in tracing up the nationality of Manasseh. He, however, committed a great error in treating the *three*
heads of the Israelitish nation as *one*, and applying the various scriptures to the
one, that should have been applied to the *three*, but mainly to Judah, which drove
him to the irresistable conclusion that the United States was to be perpetual,
and was the antitypical Israel of the Bible. The prophecies that give perpetuity
to the final or last form of God's government on earth, are numerous; but they
must not be placed to the credit of Manasseh or Ephraim, but to Judah; for all
under the first heads pass away, and the three must reappear and ultimate in *one*,
under Judah as head. In this alone is to be realized all that is promised of true
earthly greatness, nationally speaking. But I am forestalling my reader, and
will return to Israel under Manasseh, and give some very distinctive marks of *his*
Israel, not mentioned by Mr. Baldwin.

In the division and settlement of the children of Israel, in the land of promise,
we find the land very definitely and circumspectly laid off into thirteen States
geographically. After Manasseh's portion was defined in 16 ch. Joshua, we find
in 17 ch: 5 v. that "ten portions fell to Manasseh, beside the land of Gilead and
Bashan, which were on the other side Jordan," making just thirteen, (for the
East side was divided into three lots,) five of which were female portions. See
same ch. 3 and 4 v. So that the whole land, thus divided into thirteen lots, three
of which were on the East side of Jordan, and ten on the West, is taken as the
type of or *number* of Manasseh's kingdom. One of the most distinctive marks
was the *five female* lots, or states, to be found in it. Please turn to the original
thirteen of 1776, and see if you will not find five of them to be female ; and if so,
does not this settle the point of its identity at once, and remove all doubt? North
Carolina, South Carolina, Virginia, Maryland and Massachusetts. With the
foregoing, together with what Mr. Baldwin has said to the point, and it is very
much indeed, we will rest the matter, for the present at least ; holding ourself
ready at any future leisure (which we have not now,) to give much additional
scripture, of the same nature, in proof of our position.

Having, with the assistance of Mr. Baldwin, traced up the three great typical
nations of Ephraim, Judah and Manasseh—the two first to their end, as types—
we may expect the third to end likewise ; and, from present indications, the time
draweth near. For immediately after the first Israel added royalty to its government, it began to grow weak and topple to its fall ; and, indeed, may be said
to have fallen at the death of its first king;—for after that event there remained
but the semblance of a government;—and, immediately thereafter, we find the
sovereign and independent State of Judah seceded from the old confederacy, and

set up house keeping for herself, and successfully resisted coercion until her independence was acknowledged by the whole house of Israel, who came down to Hebron and confederated with her ; and she then reigned over the whole of Judah and Israel seventy-three years. Have we anything corresponding with this in our history, and in our day? Need we call attention to what followed the election of the first *king* of the United States? (Which is Manasseh's kingdom, or modern Sodom.) We find the same leaven of states-rights is set in rapid action; and "Judah's seven" secede from the new confederacy, and the building of the new Jerusalem commences under the gracious promise that "Jerusalem shall be inhabited as towns without walls, for the multitude of men and cattle therein, for I, saith the Lord, will be unto her a wall of fire, round about ; and will be the glory in the midst of her ; and the Lord shall inherit Judah his portion in the holy land, and shall choose Jerusalem again." We close for the present, for want of time ; but if, through the wisdom and mercy of the "King of Kings and Lord of Lords,' we are spared until next spring, we shall resume; and have something to say of the anti-types of the three typical kingdoms here mentioned; and especially much to say of our beloved *Confederate States of America*, as found in the Bible. For the present, adieu !

  OCTOBER, 1863.

CHAPTER SEVENTH.

WE resume (April 1st, 1864,) our task, left off in October, 1863, for want of leisure, and will try to redeem our promise, then made ; and will first call attention to the fact that God's chosen people made *three* distinct periods of conquest of the heathen nations whose land they were to possess, and *three* distinct settlements of the same, at *three* distinct periods of time ; and that the two first settlements consisted each of *three* tribes, and the last settlement of *seven* tribes. Now, we assume that the first settlement of three, type or represent that the nation should have three national heads, under its first or typical dispensation ; and, further, as the first set of threes was not in the promised land of Canaan—but was on the East side of Jordan—that this fact indicates that the national heads they represent would not reach the promised land of *national* rest: that the stormy political Jordon was yet between them and that rest. The first tribe, in first set of threes, is Reuben and stands for the first kingdom of Israel, which we have shown was Ephraim ; the second tribe, in the first set of threes, is Gad, and stands for the second confederate head, under Judah or David ; and the third tribe, in said set, was Manasseh, and represents the third confederate head, under Manasseh, which is the United States of America. Having gone through with the first set of threes, we will now examine the character given to them : for whatever was their character, such was to be the character of the confederate heads that they severally represent; and the heads must appear chronologically, as the tribal settlers named. Reuben was not to excel, though he was the *beginning* of strength : he was as unstable as water: and was withal a leacherous son, and the first born. Was not that the character of the *first born* kingdom of Israel, under Ephraim? Though it "was the might and the *beginning* of national strength,' the excellency of dignity, and the excellency of power, it was too unstable to excel; too leacherous to retain its purity, as Joshua left it. Need I add more of this head of the nation? I think not ; as all Bible readers well know how unstable and corrupt it became, very soon after Joshua's death, and ever remained unstable. Next in order is Gad. It is said of him that "A troop should overcome him: but he should overcome at last." "Blessed be he that enlargeth Gath : he dwelleth as a lion, and teareth the arm with the crown of the head : he provided the first part for himself, because there is a portion of the lawgiver was he seated: and he came with the heads of the people : he executed the justice of the Lord and his judgments with Israel." We ask : was this the character of the second head of Israel, under Judah or David? Emphatically it was. The kingdom, under David's first anointing by Samuel, *never did take* governmental form: himself, and all the semblance of a government he had about him, were fugitives from the vengeance of Saul, fleeing for protection to the land of the heathen nation of the Philistines. His government, to which he was anointed, was overcome by a troop too numerous for him; but, finally, he did overcome, and triumph most gloriously, for seventy-three years. He was said to dwell as a lion, and teareth the arm of power that had stood in his way; and with it, also, the crown of glory, from the head that had worn it, and placed it upon his own royal head. And with Judah's noted lion mark, he has, also, the law-giver feature, promised to Judah. Now, we have no scriptural evidence whatever that God ever accomplished what is here promised, or that a troop overcome him. It does not fit God; but it does the kingdom of David or Israel under Judah; and, as God is second named in the first settlement of three, and has Judah's distinctive features or marks about him, then we conclude that Judah's national head should appear second; and the fact that it did, proves our conclusion to a demonstration. The next settler, (being the third and last of the three,) was Manasseh, and represents, in *order* and *character* his own confederate head. And first: his order, or number, was third; and so must be his confederate head. Was it so? It certainly was. The United States of America was and is the *third* in the order of kingdoms that have arisen in the history of the world, of that peculiar confederate type: and as we know this cannot be disproven—or, I think, even doubted—we shall say no more upon the order of time, but shall proceed, at once, to examine the character given to Manasseh, as it is to be the character of his government.

In the settlement of the three above named tribes, on the East side of Jordan, it is said, in Numbers the xxxii ch: 33 v.: "Moses gave unto them the kingdom of the Amorite, and the kingdom of Bashan;" and 39 v. "the children of Machir the son of Manasseh went to Gilead, and took it, and dispossessed the Amorite which was in it." Here we see as soon as his inheritance is allotted to him, he exhibits his aggressive character, his energy and warlike prowess. 40th verse: 'Moses gave Gilead unto Machir the son of Manasseh; and he dwelt therein. And Jair the son of Manasseh went and took the small towns thereof. And Nobah went and took Kenath. Again, in the xvii ch. of Joshua, 1 v., it is said "Gilead and Bashan were given to Machir the son of Manasseh, *because he was a man of war*." In the 14th v. the children of Joseph (Ephraim and Manasseh,) complain to Joshua because territory enough had not been given them, claiming that they were a "great people;" and Joshua, in the 15th verse replied: "If thou be a great people, then get thee up to the wood country, and cut down for thyself there in the land of the Perizzites and of the giants, if mount Ephraim be too narrow for thee. And they in turn reply: "The hill is not enough for us." Again Joshua replies: "Thou art a great people, and hast great power. . . . . . The mountain shall be thine; for it is a wood, and thou shalt cut it down: and the *outgoings* of it shall be thine: for thou shalt drive out the Canaanites, though they have iron chariots, and though they be strong." We will add one more scripture, of character to this East side Manasseh, and will have done, for the present. See Joshua, xxii ch: 7, 8 v., where he sends them away with a blessing, thus:— "Return with much riches unto your tents, and with very much cattle, with silver, and with gold, and with brass, and with iron, and with very much raiment: divide the spoil of your enemies with your brethren." If this is not sufficient: "You would not believe, though one should arise from the dead." The applicability of all the foregoing, to the United States, is so easy, simple, and self-evident, that we might offend common apprehension by making the application. We, however, will recapitulate. Manasseh was the third settler, of first settlement; and as the third settler typed the third kingdom of Israel, in order of time and character, whatever kingdom, therefore, that possessed that peculiar confederate type, and arose after the kingdom of Israel, under David, must be the one intended by prophecy, if the character also agree, which all must see it does in the aggressive, warlike, indomitable, territory getting, energetic, greatness of the people: wealth, in silver, gold, cattle, brass, iron, very much raiment, &c. of the United States. Having thus gone through with the first formal settlements, and shown, or called attention to, the *two*, contending powers that they represent, we deem it proper, in this connection, to call attention to these same three heads, treated of in the xvi ch. of Ezekiel, (which chapter I trust all my readers will carefully examine.) Here you will see they are called the king-doms of "Jerusalem, Samaria, and Sodom;" and that they are "Sisters," and that these *sisters* have each "Daughters." So if the three *sisters* be "kingdoms," then *must* their daughters also be "kingdoms." This is again (but in another form of expression,) the nation and company of nations promised to the fathers. "The nation" is the government in its oneness, or confederate head; "the company of nations" is the same nation in its several *states*—or "Daughters." This "nation" corresponds exactly with the general government at Washington city, and the daughters to the several state governments. Who those "sisters" are, we have largely shown elsewhere; but as one of them here bears the name of "Sodom," it may be well to notice it somewhat." She is styl'd the "younger sister;" while Samaria, or the first kingdom of Israel, is called the "elder" of Jerusalem. Such we have already seen to be the fact. Samaria, or Ephraim's, was the first confederate head of Israel; then Judah or Jerusalem; and third or last, was Manasseh—United States—or "Sodom," as here called. Some will, doubtless, object, and say that reference is here had to ancient Sodom, of Abraham and Lot's day, which was destroyed by God's angel, sent for that purpose; for the scripture here says that "she committed abominations, and therefore she was taken away, or destroyed." We shall object, in turn; and claim that ancient Sodom was, in no sense, a "sister" government to Jerusalem and Samaria; and instead of being younger, she was, by many centuries, older than either. The sisterhood here spoken of did not *consist* in wickedness as is supposed by Dr. Clarke, and others; for it is said of Jerusalem, Ezekiel xvi ch. 47 v.: "Yet hast thou not walked after their ways, nor done after their abominations: but as if that were a *very little* thing, thou wast corrupted more than they in all thy ways." 48th verse: "As I live, saith the Lord God. Sodom thy sister hath not done, she nor her daughters, as thou hast done, thou and thy daughters." 51st verse: "Neither hath Samaria committed *half* of thy sins; but thou hast multiplied thine abominations more than they." This will at once prove that the kinship did not consist in the degree of wickedness. In what sense, then, was she a "sister" of the other two? or in what sense were they all three said to be sisters? We answer. All three had a common parent or author, even God who claims and calls them *his*; while he never did so call ancient Sodom; and further, they are sisters because in the peculiar type, or confederate form, of their several governments,—all being "confederate, states-rights nationalities,"—and are again necessary to make up the number three, promised. If it is objected again, that it is all this *Sodom* was "taken away" and did not exist at the time this prophecy was spoken, we simply answer, in scriptural language: "God calls those things that are not, as if though they were." And there are many instances of the same kind of expressions, "calling things that are not, as if though they were," that might be given, if needful; but we apprehend th. above will be satisfactory.

been hit off by a master hand, "to the very life." Again, in the 56th verse, it is said to Jerusalem: "Thy sister Sodom was not mentioned (or named,) by thy mouth in the day of thy pride," or excellency. Why not? For the very good reason that *she did not at that time exist.* Jerusalem knew nought of her, for she did not arise until 1760. This proves that ancient Sodom is not intended; for, doubtless, old Sodom was often in the mouth of Jerusalem. The reader will also recollect the significant fact that Washington city, and its government, has, for the last thirty years, been familiarly called "modern Sodom" in political circles; thus, as if guided by inspiration, to give her her proper or prophetic name —not knowing at the time that she was "spiritually called Sodom." Here, in this xvi chapter of Ezekiel, as in many similar presentations of this subject in the Bible, is kept in view this *three* in *one* form, and at the same time the plurality under each form of the government of God's people. "Jerusalem, and her daughters; Samaria, and her daughters; Sodom, and her daughters; corresponding, as before noticed, to the confederate heads of the people, and with the several state government of each. These three "sisters" being disposed of by the sacred historian as types, we are informed that *all three* shall return again to their former standings; and then "Samaria and Sodom" are to be given, or joined to, "Jerusalem, for daughters." 53d verse: "When I shall bring again their captivity, the captivity of Sodom and her daughters, and the captivity of Samaria and her daughters, then will I bring again the captivity of thy captives in the midst of them. . . . . . When thy sisters, Sodom and her daughters, shall return to their former estate, (standing) and Samaria and her daughters shall return to their former estate, then thou and thy daughters shall return to your former estate. . . . . . Then thou shalt remember thy ways, and be ashamed, when thou shalt *receive* thy sisters, thine elder and thy younger: and I will *give them unto thee* for daughters, but not by thy covenant." So we leave them here, —as we have done once before—holding them all as types; and shall seek for, and point out, some of the promises of their anti-types and anti-type; for they are each a type of themselves, as three, and also of themselves as one, after the confederation under Jerusalem, as just quoted above. These have all been, in part, realizing nationalities; and have been so, progressively, from the first to the last. Ephraim was first, or "elder;" "was the beginning of strength and excellency;" but only the beginning. He realizes or effects least of the three; he was too corrupt and unstable. Judah, or Jerusalem, succeeds him, (after a hard struggle, in which, at first, he was overcome,) and becomes much more realizing than Ephraim. and seemed to bid fair to accomplish all that was to have been expected, under the oft-repeated promises to the Fathers and Patriarchs. Witness the triumphs of David's, and the wisdom and splendor of Solomon's reigns; yet he, too, passed away: showing, thus, that he, like Ephraim, was a type; and as Ephraim typed him, he, in turn, must type his successor and brother, Manasseh, Sodom, the "younger," or United States of 1776,—which nation, in the short space of eighty-four years has accomplished more, under God, her author, for the general emancipation and advancement, or elevation; or, in short, for the political redemption of the earth, than all others put together, since the world began;—so Jacob, the third father of national promise, accomplished more, nationally, as before remarked. than Abraham and Isaac. But as he was a brother of the two preceding nations, and settled first on the East side of Jordan, and not in the promised land of Canaan, (as they also had done by representatives,) he also was a type, and must pass away; and as he is now rapidly dissolving, Judah the *first settler*, of the second *three* tribes, and on the *West* side of Jordan, *strictly within* the promised land of Canaan—Judah, the *final* and realizing head of God's ancient people: Judah, the beloved of the Lord; Judah, the mount Zion of his choice, appears, looming up, majestically, from the political horizon. *She was born in a day*, according to the prophecy of Isaiah lxvi ch: 8 v.; and that, too, without labor pains, or previous travailing pangs. Verse 7th: "Before she travailed, she brought forth; before her pain came, she was delivered of a man child." Now, this man child, in the 8th verse is said to be a nation, and to have been born at once; born in a day. 8th verse: "Who hath heard such a thing? who hath seen such things? Shall the earth be made to bring forth in one day? shall a *nation* be *born at once?*" Such an event had never occurred before: had not so much as been "heard of:" it was an anomaly in nature. Now, the question is : who is personated by the personal pronoun "she." In 7th verse, that gave birth to the man child, or n tion, before she commenced travailing? for there was an actual existence a real something, that could conceive, hold within itself, and bring forth a national reality as this man child was. Then if it was capable of bringing forth a nation, it must, itself, have been a nation ; and if so, what nation? We know of but one instance of a pangless national birth; and the scripture quoted implies that there *never was* but one ; and that one was given birth to by the *United States*, who is afterwards said to "travail :" and has she not been in travail, of the most excessive kind, ever since she gave us birth? but to no purpose of delivery, for herself, so far as we are able to see, at present; but eventually Ephraim and Manasseh will be the result of her labor pangs. "She" and ' earth." in the 7th and 8th verses, then, are the same person; and, as before said, is the United States. Who, then, is it that is said to have brought forth her *children*—a plural number—as soon as she commenced travailing? It is said to be "Zion;" and as the whole subject is upon national travail and births, "Zion" is a nation, and a nation in travail, and bringing forth, must be bringing forth nations,here called children. She is also called Jerusalem,in the 10th v. God says, in the 9th v.:"Shall I bring to the birth,and not cause to bring forth? saith the Lord; shall I cause to bring forth,and shut the womb? saith the Lord." No, verily: as God has brought us to our birth, as a nation, and caused Zion (the Confederate States,) to bring forth her children. He has said He will not close, or shut up, the womb ; but that births after births shall flow apace. God, in mercy, end our pangs of travail ; and let us, henceforth, have peaceful, pangless, national births into our Confederacy ! 10th verse : "Rejoice ye with Jerusalem, (on account of her safe delivery,) and be glad with her, all ye that love her: rejoice for joy with her, all ye that mourn for her : that ye may suck, and be satisfied with the breasts of her consolations. . . . for Behold, I will extend peace to her like a river, and the glory of the Gentiles like a flowing stream. ..... As one whom his mother comforteth, so will I comfort you ; and ye shall be comforted in Jerusalem; ..... and the hand of the Lord shall be known toward his servants, and his indignation toward his enemies. For, behold the Lord will come with fire, and with his chariots like a whirlwind, to render his anger with fury, and his rebuke with flames of fire. For by fire and by his sword will the Lord plead with all *flesh*." This whole affair, from beginning to ending, pertains to the *flesh*, or earth : is strictly political throughout: and so, to the end of chapter lxvi. See verse 20th, where t ey are to bring out of all nations, "to my holy mountain Jerusalem." Thus Jerusalem is called a "holy mountain ;" and is the same, the identical mountain,that Nebuchadnezzar saw, as a "stone cut out of the mountain" (that is, some particular mountain,) "without hands." In its first appearance it was a stone but soon "became a great mountain, and filled the whole earth," after dashing monarchy to atoms. This stone was, indeed, a great mountain, before it accomplished the total overthrow of monarchy, for less than a great and powerful nation could not do that thing ; yet its after greatness was to become such, that by way of contrast, it is at first called a stone, (which is only another name or figure for a government,) and afterwards a "great mountain." This "stone" is none other than the man child born without labor, in verse seven, above noticed; and the exact correspondence between, being "born without labor," and "cut out without hand," proves them to be the same nation. The hands, we all know, are the standard and undeviating symbols or signs of labor ; and as the stone was cut out without hands, it was simply accomplished "without labor,"just as the child was born, and just as the "Confederate States of America was born, or cut out of the mountain of Manasseh, or Sodom, and that, too, *in a day :* not that days of labor have not followed quickly upon the heels of birth for indeed it has, and children have been the *result ;* for I question very much whether Virginia, North Carolina, Tenne see, Kentucky, Missouri, and Arkansas would have been born into the Confederacy, as children, if "labor" had not commenced. It is not said that any births, save the man child, occurred, until travail commenced; but then it is announced "as soon," *immediately* upon travail, children are born unto her. So, if Mr. Lincoln had let us rest quiet and unmolested after our peaceful, unlaborious birth, he might have retained his fair daughters; he, otherwise, quickly lost. While upon the subject of the birth of the "man child," we will notice the birth of a "man child" that took place some eighty-four years prior to the one above. See Revelations; xii ch: "A woman clothed with the sun, and the moon under her feet, and upon her head a crown of twelve stars: and she being with child cried, travailing in birth, and pained to be delivered. . . . And she brought forth a man child, who was to rule all nations with a rod of iron." And if all nations, our nation is included, unless we can show that the nation born in lxvi ch. Isaiah, 7 v., called there a "man child," is ours and is the offspring and heir of the first man child. Mr. Baldwin has shown, to my entire satisfaction, that the nation born in the person of *this* first man child, is none other than the United States; or, as we may say, Manasseh's kingdom. Now, as the United States has not done what is here said she was to do, and never will, under her present head of number three, or third kingdom of Israel, how is the difficulty to be solved? We solve it thus: Whatever is promised in scripture to a person, we must look for its fulfillment, first, in his person; and if not fulfilled in his person, we next go down his line of descendants, personal, if the thing is personal; but if national, follow on after his nationality. Viz: if a promise is found recorded to Judah, (or a curse either,) first apply it to the individual man, Judah; if not fulfilled to the man, or is not applicable to him, then it is legitimate and proper next to apply it to the *tribe* of Judah; if still no fulfillment is found, or is inapplicable, next apply it to the kingdom of Judah, under its first head; but if no fulfillment is yet found, follow up the kingdom in its next form, and so on, until you find fulfillment; for it must, and will, take place just at the time, and in the manner, that inspiration foretold. And whatever is promised to a king, is to him as a *king*, and is always political, and may be fulfilled to him in his kingdom, or his successor. Whatever was promised David, the king, was fulfilled to him as such, and if not, it descended to his regal heirs: and as much was promised him that has not yet been fulfilled, we may look expectantly for its fulfillment under this, his kingdom under its second head, and fourth head of the Israelitish nationality, and first head of the anti-typical three. Now, as the man child born of the woman was to become the political ruler of all nations; and as the United States is proven to be the nation intended by the man child; and she has dissolved, and is rapidly passing away without receiving, in herself, fulfillment, it is legitimate to transfer the promise to her regal descendant. The question, then, is who is her national offspring? to whom has she given birth? We answer unhesitatingly, as we have before done, the Confederate States of America. If she is not our mother, we have none, and are in a sad predicament; worse than in orphanage; we are a *bastard;* and "shall not enter into the congregation of the Lord until the tenth generation;" which does not suit me at all. The old lady, I admit, is treating us rather badly; but, nevertheless, we must not deny our parentage, for thereby we lay hold on the promises unfulfilled to her. The genealogy must not be broken in upon. She gave us birth; the C. S. is her child; born without any effort or labor of hers, to be sure, but none the less a child. She is the "she" of verse 7, Isaiah lxvi; and is the mother of "Zion" of verse 8th, that was born in a day; which "Zion" immediately travails, and brings forth her children; and will continue to bring forth, until "all nations and kindred and tongues," "all fowls of every wing" shall take shelter beneath the goodly cedar of Lebanon. "This stone is to fill the whole earth." This stone under the old dispensation was "Zion," the city of David; which city was a military stronghold, a fortified position on a mount of that name that commanded the city of Jerusalem; and hence Jerusalem was so often called the "daughter of Zion," being the feminine, and more defenceless representative of the government; and the two taken together are called the "double city," or "Ariel, Arial," or the two lions of God; that is, the "lion and lioness of God." The nation represented by the foregoing names, and others that might be given, was betrothed and married to God. See xvi ch. Ezekiel, 8 v. Now when I passed by thee, and looked upon thee, behold, thy time was the time of love ; and I spread my skirt over thee, and covered thy nakedness : yea, I sware unto thee, and entered into a covenant with thee, saith the Lord God, and thou becamest mine." 13th verse: "And thou wast exceeding beautiful, and thou didst prosper into a kingdom." Thus the person addressed and married was a "kingdom," and became "renowned" and prosperous; as indeed it did, under David and Solomon; and retaining its renown in a greater or less degree until finally, for its corruption, God divorced himself from her. I chapter of Isaiah : "Thus saith the Lord, Where is the bill of your mother's divorcement, whom I have put away ?" "Behold, for your iniquities have ye sold yourselves, and for your transgressions is your mother put away." This is not his church, as is commonly supposed, but without one single ground of authority for it. To satisfy yourself, read again the xvi ch of Ezekiel. This kingdom here divorced, or put away, is then called "barren and desolate ;" and this same barren and desolate, after a time, is taken back to the bosom of God, her former husband; who says to her, Isaiah liv ch: 5 v.: "Thy maker is thine husband ; the Lord of hosts is his name ; and thy Redeemer the Holy One of Israel ; . . . for the Lord hath called thee *as a woman forsaken*" [or divorced] "and grieved in spirit, and a wife of youth, when thou wast refused:" who is now addressed, in the 1st verse, thus: "Sing, O barren, thou that didst not bear ;" [that is, during her divorcement,] "break forth into singing, and cry aloud, thou that didst not travail with child ;" [during divorcement,] "for more shall be the children of the desolate" [that was desolate, but now no longer so,] "than the children of the married wife, saith the Lord." 2d verse : "Enlarge the place of thy tent," [the country of thy dwelling,] and let them stretch forth the curtains of thine habitations : spare not, lengthen thy cords, and strengthen thy stakes ; for" [now that the womb is opened that the Lord said he would not close it again,] "thou shalt break forth [in births] on the right hand and on the left ; and thy seed shall inherit the Gentiles, and make the desolate cities to be inhabited." This is all said of "Jerusalem;" "Zion;" of the stone cut out of the mountain; of the man child of Isaiah lxvi ch.; of David's kingdom which was not to end ; of the Confederate States of America, the realization, in its beginning, of the promise to the Fathers and Patriarchs. Again, under the figure of a branch planted by the Lord, the same nationality comes up in the xi ch. of Isaiah ; there personating the great Redeemer of the world: who, in turn, personates his own nationality. The spirit of the Lord was to rest upon this government ; the spirit of wisdom, of might, of understanding, of knowledge, of judgment, equity, &c. The *political* wolf was to be changed into a lamb ; the leopard into a kid; the lion, the fatling, the calf, the bear, all to be alike; that is, the ferocious animals here personate political personages, who were no longer to exist as such, but to become meek and harmless as the domestic animals they are here said to be ranging and feeding with. 9th verse: "They shall not hurt nor destroy in all my holy mountain : for the *earth* shall be full of the knowledge of the Lord, as the waters cover the sea." Here the branch planted is shown to be a "holy mountain;" which is nothing more nor less than a holy or pure government on this *earth*, so often promised, as here repeated again, on *earth*. Christ said of himself, as is here said of him, that "he was the root and offspring" [branch] "of David, who was of Jesse." "His rest shall be glorious: and unto him shall the Gentiles seek." 11th: "And it shall come to pass in that day, that the Lord shall set his hand again the *second* time to recover the remnant of his people, which shall be left" among the heathen nations. "He shall set up an ensign for the nations, and shall assemble the outcasts of Israel, and gather together the dispersed of Judah from the four corners of the *earth*. The envy also of Ephraim shall depart, and the adversaries of Judah shall be cut off : Ephraim shall not envy Judah, and Judah shall not vex Ephraim." Here we have a *second restoration*, and must be political; for no man ever heard of a second spiritual restoration : and then the political rulers of the Israelitish nation, Ephraim and Judah, occupy so large a space in the picture, that we are forced to see the political drift of the whole of the foregoing quotations ; and further, confirmatory of the above, is the fact that immediately after this promised restoration. it is said that these nations, restored and joined, "shall fly upon the shoulders of the Philistines toward the west : they shall spoil them of the east together : they shall lay their hand" [hand is power, and being singular, shows the union of the nation at this time.] "upon Edom and Moab ; and the children of Ammon shall obey them." These are symbols of monarchy, that is everywhere said should be destroyed by God's ancient people, when restored to united nationality. The fact is again repeated in the 15th verse : "And the Lord shall utterly destroy the tongue of the Egyptian sea ; [another symbol of monarchy,] and with his mighty wind shall he shake his hand over the river." [monarchy] "and shall smite it in the seven streams.and make men go over dryshod. . . like as it was to Israel in the day that he came up out of the land of Egypt." Monarchy, as a mighty river, made up of seven rivers, stands in the way of the universal triumph of God's government. just as the Red Sea stood in the way of the children of Israel's escape from the monarchy of Egypt; and is here, as that was. to be wrought upon by a mighty wind ; and smitten also as it was ; and the result is to be the same, so far as effecting a safe passage to his people : but in this latter case, the sea was to be utterly destroyed; and corresponds exactly with the smiting of the great monarchy image of Nebuchadnezzar by "the stone cut out of the mountain without hands," utterly destroying it. and at once taking its place, and "filling the whole earth." This frequent "dashing" and "smiting" of the symbols of monarchy. in the scriptures, points significantly to the "battle of the great day" to be fought by God's ancient people, represented by their regal successors, on the mountains of Israel. after their union or confederation with Judah: between whom there existed, for a time, a breach, or broken state, as indeed it now does. This battle is none other than "Armageddon,' now soon to be fought ; but not until the North, as "Samaria and Sodom." are given and joined to the new Jerusalem, or Confederate States, and we all become one mighty nation again ; more mighty by having been broken for a time.

Upon the restoration and re-building of Judah or Jerusalem. Zechariah is very full and explicit : opening his book upon that very subject. In its first sense his restoration has direct reference to the return of the Jews from their seventy years captivity, under Babylon; their re building of their city, temple, &c.; all of which is typical. Haggai prophecied at the same time, to encourage the people in their work ; and in connection with Zechariah, we shall notice some things he says upon the subject. They both lived and wrote during the time of said return and re-building; and where they say anything upon that subject, in its first sense, it has reference to those events then transpiring ; but when not true of the nation under that restoration, (which much was not, that was spoken by the various prophets.) then the reference is to the "latter day," or grand and final restoration of God's people to nationality. What is here said of Zerubbabel, the Governor under whose administration this typical restoration took place, —as well as what is said of Joshua, the High Priest—must be considered as typical, also. We believe there is no diversity of opinion. among our learned commentators, in saying that very much. and the more important part of what was said and promised the Jews, on their return from the Babylonish captivity, was not realized by them ; and hence we conclude that said restoration was only a typical one : land, names and all. So we shall make use of them as such. Haggai is directed by the Lord to say to Zerubbabel, the Governor ; Joshua, the High Priest; and to the people : " Be strong, and work ; for I am with you, saith the Lord." "The glory of this latter house shall be greater than of the former, saith the Lord of hosts." This was not true of the temple built at this time, and so must refer to another house. yet to be built. Again Haggai is directed to "speak to Zerubbabel, governor of Judah, saying, I will shake the heavens and the earth; and I will overthrow the throne of kingdoms, and I will destroy the strength of the kingdoms of the heathen ; and I will overthrow the chariots, and those that ride in them. . . . In that day, saith the Lord of hosts, will I take thee, O Zerubbabel, my servant, and make thee as a signet: for I have chosen thee, saith the Lord of hosts." These things were not done or accomplished under the rule of Zerubbabel, who was made a signet or seal, that they should be done ; and as the signet or seal of promise, which was with God equivalent to an oath, passed away, without the things promised being fulfilled, we are justified in saying.that Zerubbabel, the signet or seal, was typical of the true Zerubbabel that should arise, and accomplish the mission of his type. We will now notice some things that Zechariah says, relative to the same events. I will pass by chapters i, ii, iii, though very full and interesting. I do hope and trust that my reader will keep his Bible close at hand, so as he may read the prophecies we refer to and copy from; and especially on the present occasion. Chapter iv.: "And the angel that talked with me came again, and waked me. . . . and said unto me, What seest thou? And I said, I have looked, and behold a candlestick all of gold, with a bowl upon the top of it, and his seven lamps thereon, and seven pipes to the seven lamps, which are upon the top thereof : And two olive trees by it, one upon the right side of the bowl, and the other upon the left side thereof. So I answered and spake to the angel that talked with me, saying, What are these, my lord ? . . . Then he answered and spake unto me, saying, This is the word of the Lord unto Zerubbabel," [the builder] saying, Not by might, nor by power, but by my spirit, saith the Lord of hosts.' Now mark, carefully the foregoing. Zechariah sees a candlestick of seven branches, and two olive trees : he does not know what they signify, and asks the angel for their meaning. The angel answers his question by giving the Lord's words of commission and instructions to Zerubbabel, who he had sent to re-build Jerusalem ; in short, to superintend the restoration of the Jewish nation; saying further, for the encouragement of the builders, and the people: "Who art thou, O great mountain? that is, any opposing obstacle; but, more specifically, Monarchy—who, as a mountain, had ever stood in the way of God's states-rights national? "before Zerubbabel thou shalt become a plain ; and he shall bring forth the head stone thereof with shoutings, crying, Grace, grace unto it." No obstacles could defeat Zerubbabel in his work, for it was not by his might or power that he was forward ; but by the Spirit of the Lord. "Moreover the word of the Lord came unto me, saying, The hands of Zerubbabel have laid the foundation of this house; his hands shall also finish it ; and thou shalt know [hereby] that the Lord of hosts hath sent me unto you." Do not forget that this is given in explanation of the seven golden candlesticks. But we have not done with the meaning given by the angel. 10th verse : "For who hath despised the day of small things ?, The day of small things has direct reference to this house, under the typical restoration, before noticed. If any are disposed to think lightly of this former house, or day of small things, let them be assured that this "latter day" house will be transcendantly more glorious, and never ending, being the anti-type of the former. "For they shall rejoice, and shall see the plummet in the hand of Zerubbabel with those seven ; they [Zerubbabel and the seven,] are the eyes of the Lord, which run to and fro through the whole earth." Here ends the angel's explanation of the candlestick of seven branches; and it was satisfactory to the prophet for he asks no more about it. His next wishes to know what the two olive trees signify, and is told that they are "The two anointed ones, that stand by the Lord of the whole earth," being synonymous with "the two witnesses" that were slain for three days and a half ; which was shown to be the dual Israel of God, or his people in Church and State. Now, what do you understand by this seven-branched candlestick, as explained by the angel? I understand him to say, as plain as need be, that this candlestick is the house of Judah, that Zerubbabel was set to restore, or build ; and that no opposing force could stop the building ; that as his hands had laid the foundation, in the type, his hands should also finish, in the anti-type, what was begun in the type. and that the builder, Zerubbabel, in the anti-type, should be assisted by seven builders; answering to the seven States that organized the Confederate States, at Montgomery. And Jeff. Davis is the Zerubbabel of this new Jerusalem, as the seven States are as counsellors. The C. S. is the stone; and the seven States, as here called, are the seven eyes engraved thereon by the finger of God. No matter what may be the actual number of eyes or states, or yet branches to this golden candlestick, she first appears under that number, by which she is to be identified. We would like to go through this Prophet, with the reader, for our mutual benefit, but must defer it for the present, as our limits—made very limited, for want of printing facilities—forbid. It may be proper here to notice the fact that John the Revelator, mentions a similar candlestick, as the one above; and that it is said to represent the seven churches to which the address, in the first of his book, is delivered. This is all just as it should be. There are two of those candlesticks mentioned. One of them represents the Israel of God in Church; and the other one represents the very same Israel in State, or nationally. There were "two olive trees," "two candlesticks," "two prophets or teachers," "two witnesses," &c., which are all synonymous terms, and mean one and the same things; that is, the dual Israel of God ;—God's people in Church and State.

CHAPTER NINTH.

THE xxxvii of Ezekiel, from the 1st verse to the 14th inclusive, introduces us to the whole house of Israel as not only a disrupted, but as a dead and buried nation ; and spoken at the time, too, of the actual state above referred to. This is the familiar "vision of the valley of dry bones;" which, in its sequel, verses 12, 13, and 14, brings them to national life again, united as one ; as the address was to the "whole house," and called, as before, God's people. "Behold, O my people, I will open your graves, and cause you to come up out of your graves, and bring you into the land of Israel. And ye shall know that I am the Lord when I have opened your graves, O my people, and brought you up out of your graves, and shall put my spirit in you, and ye shall live, and I shall place you in your own land : then shall ye know that I the Lord have spoken and performed it, saith the Lord." The "house of Israel" was one, and the "house of Judah" was one; but the "whole house of Israel" was Jacob's twelve sons, their descendants or regal representatives. All of Israel were not Jews ; but one tribe only bore that name, and individuals of other tribes that affiliated with them; yet all Jews were Israelites ; hence, we should be careful to distinguish between the "two families" of Israel. One was Joseph's house, and embraced all Israel as natural descendants of Jacob, who was called Israel "because he had power with God and man, and had prevailed;" and Joseph's was the birthright, and as such he inherited the paternal name ; for it was to be kept up by some one, and that one of course was the birthright son. Judah's "house" was instituted and kept separate from, though within, the house of Joseph, for the specific benefit (or use, if you like it better,) of the promised Messiah or Shiloh ; for it was said of Judah Shiloh should come, and of Judah he did come ; and in and over Judah began, in initial, his reign as king, in the person of his regal father, David. We return, to consider the foregoing promise to the "whole house of Israel" of national restoration; and as no such restoration took place under the old dispensation; and as Mr. Baldwin has shown satisfactorily, with some additional proofs by ourself, in another part of our pamphlet, that Israel has been restored under this latter day dispensation, we will claim at once that the above promise found its full realization in the rise of the "whole house" of Israel or United States; and as there was no promise of perpetuity annexed to this restoration, we take it for granted that permanency was not to be expected, when not even implied ; in fact, that dissolution was and is inevitable. where God has not said, in plain terms, to the contrary; for all of the promises of final restoration are strongly marked and fortified by "everlasting," and "eternal." And what are the facts in the above case? See the 15th verse: "The word of the Lord came again unto Ezekiel, saying." This is another prophecy, by the word coming "again" at another time. It might have been the same day or hour, or year afterwards ; it matters not. And what was that word? Verse 16th says: "Take thee one stick, and write upon it, For Judah, and for the children of Israel his companions : then take another stick, and write upon it. For Joseph, the stick of Ephraim, and all the house of Israel his companions ; and join them one to another into one stick ; and they shall become one in thine hand." Now, what does all this joining of national sticks together mean, if it does not say, as plain as language can say, that the "whole house of Israel" restored in the 12th, 13th, and 14th verses, are now disjointed, broken or dissolved? and be is here set to heal the breach, to join the sticks again. Now turn to the xi ch. of Zechariah, and learn how this stick was 'cut apart." He tells us; but Ezekiel does not. It was no part of his business to do so. He was ordered to unite them: after which to explain to the people the meaning. 21st verse : "Thus saith the Lord God: Behold, I will take the children of Israel [the whole house,] from among the heathen, ... and will make them one nation in the land upon the mountains of Israel ; and one king shall be king to them all : and they shall be no more two nations, neither shall they be divided into two kingdoms any more at all. ... I will save them out of all their dwelling-places, wherein they have sinned, and will cleanse them : so shall they be my people, and I will be their God. And David my servant shall be king over them ; and they all shall have one shepherd : they shall also walk in my judgments, and observe my statutes, and do them. And they shall dwell in the land that I have given unto Jacob my servant, wherein your fathers have dwelt ; and they shall dwell therein, even they, and their children, and their children's children for ever: and my servant David shall be their prince forever. Moreover, I will make a covenant of peace with them ; it shall be an everlasting covenant with them ; and I will place them, and multiply them, and will set my sanctuary in the midst of them for evermore. *My tabernacle also shall be with them:* yea. I will be their God. and they shall be my people. And the heathen shall know that I the Lord do sanctify Israel, *when my sanctuary shall be in the midst of them for evermore.*" This promise remains to be fulfilled; but the beginning of its fulfillment—the joining of the sticks—the union of the North with the South—is close at hand. It cannot be claimed that this refers to a restoration in the Holy Land, or Palestine, because of the expressions "*land given to Jacob,*" "*wherein your fathers dwell,* &c.; for if such expressions are not figures, neither is "David my servant" a figure, but real, which would necessitate the resurrection to life of King David, who has been dead over two thousand years. Such conclusions would be the heighth of absurdity. The old land, names, kings, &c., are taken to type or represent the new. The nation here restored is Israel, under Judah, and the names of her ancient fathers, kings and country are hers by *inheritance*; and who has any right to complain ? besides, God said to David that he would appoint another land, and plant them in it. Second Samuel, vii ch., God says to David, 10 v.: ' Moreover I will appoint a place for my people Israel, and will plant them, that they may dwell in a place of their own, and move no more ; neither shall the children of wickedness afflict them any more, as beforetime." If stronger proof of a *new national land*, and a new planting therein, is wanted, we fear we shall not be able to give it, and shall not attempt to do so; but while upon this head of planting, we will give some other passages, that speak of national planting, and national plants. Jeremiah xxiii, 5 v. says: "Behold, the days come, saith the Lord, that I will raise unto David a righteous Branch, [nation] and a King [called David,] shall reign and prosper, and shall execute judgment and justice in the earth. In his days Judah shall be saved, and Israel shall dwell safely." xxxiii ch. 15 v.. "In those days, and at that time, will I cause the Branch of righteousness to grow up unto David. ... David shall never want a man to sit upon the throne of the house of Israel." Zechariah iii ch. 8v.: "For behold I will bring forth my servant, the Branch; for behold the *stone* that I have laid before Joshua, upon one stone seven eyes." Here, as elsewhere, the "stone" appears as a nation or branch of David; and on this occasion it has seven eyes. The Confederacy being the Branch—immediately explained to be a *stone*, and said to have seven eyes, which are the seven States in its first organization—is the identical stone cut out of the mountain without hands. Isaiah, lx ch., beginning at the 5th verse, is a life size picture of the C S ; after Samaria and Sodem "flow into" it: which ci.

closes thus: "Thy people also shall be all righteous : they shall inherit the land forever, the branch of my planting, the work of my hands, that I may be glorified. A little one shall become a thousand, and a small one a strong *nation.*" Here you see it is a nation again. In the xvii ch. of Ezekiel a parable, which is further called a riddle, was put to the house of Israel, saying: "A great eagle with great wings, long winged, full of feathers, which had divers colours, came unto Lebanon, and took the highest branch of the cedar," and planted, &c.; explained in the 12th, 13th, and 14th verses to be the taking of the king and people of Jerusalem captive, by the king of Babylon, who planted them in his own land ; and also planting a subject kingdom at Jerusalem. When done with this planting of the king of Babylon, God says, 22nd verse: "I will *also* take of the highest *branch* of the high cedar, and will set it; I will crop off from the top of his young twigs a tender one, and will plant it upon an high mountain and eminent: In the mountain of the height of Israel will I plant it ; and it shall bring forth boughs, and bear fruit, and be a goodly *cedar:* and under it shall dwell all fowl of every wing: in the shadow of the branches thereof shall they dwell." Here God says he would do what the king of Babylon had done; and Isaiah, as just quoted above, shows that God had done it. The "little plant was to become a thousand;" the small one a "strong nation." Now, when and where did these *two* plantings take place? The first "I will also take of the highest branch of the high cedar, and will set it," occurred in 1776, and corresponds with the man child of Revelation, that was to rule all nations with a rod of iron; so its locality its known hereby, as well as from the date. The second planting "I will crop off from [as the stone was cut out of the mountain,] the top of his young twigs a tender one, and will plant it." This *second* slip for planting was taken off from the *first.* and was young and tender. Young and tender imply feebleness; wanting in physical powers; cut from the tender growing top, and not from near the root of power. It had no root attached at planting. This fits to a scribe; touches everywhere. The seven seceding States sat, over two thousand years ago, for this faithful likeness. Next the place of planting : "Upon a high mountain, and eminent in the mountain of the height of Israel, will I plant it." As the whole planting affair, from the king of Babylon on to this last and final one, was national; and as a mountain is a very common symbol of a nation; and as a nation could not be planted upon an isolated pile of earth, it follows that this planting of a nation was "upon" a nation, or in a nation. Now, if the C. S. have not been planted in the United States, I am not able to give her geographical position ; and if, after all our labor, we cannot locate her, our toiling has been in vain. It was only severed from the parent stock, and took root where it was, just as the stone was severed by incision from the mountain; the knife of secession simply passed between the parent stock and the tender one, leaving it, as to local position, untouched, and having and retaining its vitality in a genial clime and favorable soil, it could not fail to take root, as it did in organization, at Montgomery, Ala.; and then to grow, and shall continue to do so, until "It shall bring forth boughs, and bear fruit, and be a goodly *cedar;* and under it shall dwell all fowl of every wing; in the shadow of the branches thereof shall they dwell." "And all the trees of the field [all the nations of the earth] shall know that I the Lord have brought down the high tree, [U. S.] have exalted the low tree [C. S.] have dried up the green tree. [U. S.] and have made the dry tree [C. S.] to flourish." We might continue similar quotations and remarks; but our time and space forbids. We will now call attention to what followed immediately upon the "joining of the sticks," the "flowing together" of those that had been apart; of the "mending of the breach," &c., by which joining, healing, flowing together, the divided nation became one, "never more to be divided into two kingdoms," but to remain "one nation in the land upon the mountains of Israel." What followed this re-union? Answer : The "destruction of the Egyptian sea," or monarchy, called again a river of "*seven streams*," Isaiah xi ch: 15th and 16th v. In the xxxvii ch. of Ezekiel, as we have quoted, this union of the nation took place. It is immediately followed, in the xxxviii and xxxix ch., with the total and final overthrow of monarchy by the hands of the nation so restored upon the moun-

tains of Israel; and as this is the great battle of "Armageddon," we will call
attention to the fact that monarchy is represented in that battle by seven nations
confederated or banded together for our overthrow. See Z. 3, 5, and 6 vs., of
38 ch. Ezekiel. There "Gog is the chief priest of Meshech and Tubal; and with them
are Persia, Ethiopia, Libya, Gomer, Togarmah. Here the great river of monarchy
is called Gog, and his seven streams that flow into him are found in the seven
nations here named as joined with him in this unsuccessful battle, on their part,
but most gloriously successful on our part. Isaiah had said that this river should
be "smitten in its seven streams, and dried up;" but he did not particularize or
tell us how: but Ezekiel, in these two chapters, does. Please read both Prophets
as referred to above; we have not space to copy. We have, in this chapter, said
that Zechariah, in his xi chapter, tells how the sticks of Joseph and Judah came
to be separate, or cut apart, and thus became two nations. It is conceded by all
that this chapter most certainly tells us of the division of the Israelitish people
into two separate kingdoms; but when or how, the most learned are at a loss to
determine. Bishop Newcom says he could not explain the passage in reference
to said division, without supposing the united nation to exist at the time the
Prophet wrote this prophecy, which he very well knew was not the fact; for it
was spoken many generations after the house of Joseph, or the ten tribes, had
broken off from the house of Judah; and spoken, in fact, when Judah was in the
act of returning from her captivity, and was actually then re-building Jerusalem
and the temple. The learned commentator Mr. Joseph Meal, says: "Methinks
such a prophecy was not seasonable for Zechariah's time, when the city yet, for
a great part, lay in her ruins, and the temple had not yet recovered hers; nor
was it agreeable to the scope of Zechariah's commission; who, together with his
colleague, Haggai, was to encourage the people, lately returned from captivity, to
build their temple and to re-organize their commonwealth." So you will see the
most profoundly learned were left in the dark as to the proper understanding of
this prophecy. Upon a similar prophecy, detailing the very same events, Dr. Clarke
says, in substance : "This prophecy was spoken by some unknown prophet, who
lived before the ten tribes broke off from the house of Judah ; for it has reference to
that event, and could not have been spoken by the prophet in whose book it is
here recorded, for he lived and wrote long after that event; and in compiling or
making up this latter prophet's record, this prophecy of some unknown prophet, by
mistake got into the wrong book." Is not this a strange way of getting clear of
a difficulty, not then solvable ? "its time not having come." The fact is, this prophecy has direct reference to the present existing state of things in the "latter day
Israel," and could not have been understood until the present time ; but its time
of revealment having come, there is now no difficulty in the matter, even by the
unlearned We find this prophecy, as it stands in the xi ch. of Zechariah, totally
wanting in chronology, or order of time as to the things or events spoken of.
This, however, is no uncommon occurrence, and presents little difficulty. We will
endeavor to give it chronologically; give it in the order in which the events or actions severally occur. The whole nation is treated as a " flock," and a part of
them are called "the flock of slaughter," being appointed to death, the weaker
by the stronger, who are called their possessors, "who slay them." This flock of
slaughter, called also "poor of the flock;" that is, the weak or more defenseless
(humanly speaking,) of the whole flock or nation, we understand to have reference to the South, as a whole, and to all, North and South, individually, who are
with the South in sentiment and sympathy, and as such, subject themselves to
the wrath of the North. This flock of slaughter claims our first attention. 4th
verse: "Thus saith the Lord my God; Feed [or sustain] the flock of the slaughter;
whose possessors [the North] slay them, and hold themselves not guilty: and
they [the North] that sell them say, Blessed be the Lord; for I am rich." How
true, all know that will reflect for but a moment. The North has indeed grown
rich, almost beyond measure, by buying and selling the South at her own price;
asking us no questions about the matter. We have literally been her possession :
she was literally slaying us, and had well nigh accomplished the thing, before
we were aroused to a sense of our danger; and for all this, she hypocritically and

sanctimoniously says,—"Blessed be the Lord!" claiming, hereby, that under God's authority they have done this wickedness—as we all know they do to this day, by their thanksgivings for any seeming success over us. The poor flock being thus provided for. God says: "I will no more pity the inhabitants of the land, [that is, the North,] but, lo, I will deliver the men every one into his neighbor's hand, and into the hand of his king : [that is, into the hands of the South,] and they [the South,] shall smite the land out of their [the North's] hand and I will not deliver them, [the North.] And I will feed the flock of slaughter, even you, O poor of the [original] flock;" thus re-assuring us of his guardian care and protection. Thus prefacing what he designed doing, he then, proparatory to the action, takes two staves or sticks, one called Beauty, and the other called Bands. Beauty represented God's covenant with the whole house of Israel; and now, as he designed to break the brotherhood, it was very proper that he should first dissolve the covenant between himself and them. So he says, verse 10 : "And I took my staff, Beauty, and cut it asunder, that I might break my covenant, which I had made with *all* the people. And it was broken in that day : and so the poor of the flock [South] that waited upon me knew that it was the word [or will] of the Lord," that it should be so; and so we do consider and receive it. Now that the covenant between God and the whole nation, or Israel as one, is broken or cut asunder, we are ready for cutting the band between the brotherhood, which follows at once, but could not have gone before. The brotherhood could not have been disabled so long as God's covenant remained with the whole house. 14th verse: "Then I cut asunder mine other staff, Bands, that I might break the brotherhood between Judah and Israel, [Joseph.] Thus; the North and South were separated; and in immediate connection with this breaking of the brotherhood, is announced the raising up of a foolish Shepherd or ruler in the land of the North, (that land that was before said should be smitten out of the hands of those that then held possession or rule,) which foolish Shepherd, it is said "Shall not visit those that be cut off, neither shall seek the young one, nor heal that that is broken, nor feed that that standeth still : but he [the Shepherd] shall eat the flesh of the fat and tear their claws in pieces" Abe Lincoln sat for this faithful likeness many generations ago. He did not visit or seek the young cedar of Lebanon that had been cut off by the knife of secession, in a spirit calculated to bring them back and heal the breach in the brotherhood. So far was he from "healing that that was broken," that he did not so much as feed, strengthen, or encourage those that had as yet stood still in the matter, to hope for better things at the shepherd's hands. "Hope deferred maketh the heart sick or faint;" they could stand still no longer; he forced the fatal knife to descend again and again, until Virginia, North Corolina, Tennessee, Kentucky, Missouri and Arkansas. are all found in motion. What is further said of this foolish Shepherd ? why. that, instead of feeding and giving of strength and hope for the cut off and the standing still. "He shall eat the flesh of the fat and tear their claws [or means of defence] in pieces." What is promised him for this ? "Woe to the idle Shepherd that leaveth the flock! the sword shall be upon his arm. and upon his right eye : his arm shall be clean dried up, and his right eye shall be utterly darkened." Woe, to old Abe! Chronologically, the three first verses cover the same actions as the cutting of the staff called Bands, which was the breaking of the brotherhood of Judah and Joseph. The nation is addressed as "Lebanon," and ordered to throw open her doors, that the fire might enter, and devour the cedars of Lebanon. So if Lebanon represents the Nation, the cedars must represent the States. "Open thy doors, O Lebanon, [U. S.] that the fire [political burning,] may devour thy cedars. [States.] Howl, fir tree; [less excellent nations,] for the cedar [the most excellent tree or U. S.] is fallen ; because the mighty are spoiled : howl, O ye oaks of Bashan ; [less excellent nations,] for the forest of the vintage [U. S.] is come down. There is a voice of the howling of the shepherds ; [Governors of the Northern States,] for their glory [the Union,] is spoiled : a voice of the roaring of young lions; [chief persons] for the pride of Jordan [the Union,] is spoiled." The next thing that claims our attention, as well as the next in order of time, or chronologically is the statement

"And I fed the flock," that is the "flock of slaughter," or poor flock; which we may *at this time* was the C. S., in organic form : before this time, we spoke of them as the South. Soon after the feeding begins, a mutual loathing and abhorring is found to exist between three of the Shepherds fed, and the feeder, who is none other than God ; and consequently God cuts off these three Shepherds from his flock, and says to them : "I will not feed you : that that dieth let it die ; and that that is to be cut off, let it be cut off;" no use in delaying the matter, as there was a mutual loathing ; and so they were cut off "in one month." These three Shepherds must represent three States, belonging, at the time, to the Confederacy: and if so, they are Tennessee, Kentucky, and Missouri. We have thus noticed this prophecy because applicable strictly to the present state of things in Modern Israel, and not to any prior time. It tells of secession and the Confederacy as plain as can be. We will cite one more passage to prove that Israel, restored in the latter day, would dissolve or disunite. In the xiii ch. of Isaiah Babylon the ancient and unrelenting foe of God's national Israel, was taken up by the Prophet, and a burden or curse pronounced against her, and her total overthrow detailed, with promises to his own people of deliverance from their bondage. Chapter xiv : "For the Lord will have mercy on Jacob, and will yet choose Israel, and set them in their own land : and the strangers [negroes] shall be joined with them, and they [the negroes,] shall cleave to the house of Jacob. And the people shall take them, and bring them to their place : [the place that God said to David he would appoint and plant his people in it, and that they should no more remove or be afflicted as aforetime.] and the house of Israel shall possess them in the land of the Lord for *servants and handmaids :* and they shall take them captives, whose captives they were ; and they shall rule over their oppressors." The Egyptians, the descendants of Ham are here had reference to, who had enslaved the Israelites for so long a period, while in Egypt ; but now the tables are to be turned, and the former masters to become the slaves, and the former slaves to become the masters. "And it shall come to pass in the day that the Lord shall give thee rest from thy sorrow, and from thy fear, and from the hard bondage wherein thou wast made to serve, [in Babylon,] that thou shalt take up this parable against the king of Babylon, and say, How hath the oppressor ceased! the golden city ceased! The Lord hath broken the staff of the wicked, and the sceptre of the rulers." This parable of rejoicing, on the part of Israel, over fallen Babylon, is kept up, to the 29th verse inclusive; but the Prophet, in the 29th v. admonishes them not to rejoice, as a *whole,* because the rod of Babylon was broken, for there was in store for them *dissolving* evils. "Rejoice not thou, *whole Palestina,* because the rod of him that smote thee, is broken : *for out of the serpent's root shall come forth a cockatrice, and his* [the cockatrice's] *fruit shall be a fiery flying serpent."* So the old serpent Babylon, that spawn of the devil, Monarchy, properly called a serpent after its sire, is not dead yet ; has vitality in her very roots. We rejoiced at our deliverance from her a little, just a little, too soon. The revolution of '76 gave us rest, and seeming security, for a time ; and we, naturally enough, rejoiced and took up a parable against monarchy in general, and taunted them on every suitable occasion. But in the mean time her roots were germinating secretly, and out of sight, that serpent of serpents, that has glisken cockatrice and bane of States-rights, confederate republics—called *"centralism,"* tending directly to the *one man power* principle, in opposition to God, who alone is *one in power.* "Centralism" does not make an open and direct attack, but gives birth to a *"fiery flying serpent;"* which, for want of a better name, we will call *".Abolitionism."* This spawn of Centralism came across the waters in the guise of a messenger of Christ, and at once entered and desecrated the sacred desk; and thus, unsuspectingly, got at the people, and won upon them, as a wolf in sheep's clothing would, naturally, upon the sheep. And the sheep, headed by their Shepherds, soon set up a bleating to Congress; but in their said bleatings, they said not one word in opposition to *"States rights,"* nor one word in favor of Centralism. No! not they. Their calling and mission was a higher one. They did not wish or care to *"dabble"* in politics. Let the nation take care of itself, and they would take care of the souls. But as soon as they acquire a little strength, and organize. they become bolder, and begin to clamor most vociferously, but not against State Sovereignty; that must be kept in the back ground until strength to strike boldly, and confident of certain success, is obtained. The sequel I need not write ; it is already written on the broad face of our whole land, in fire and blood. The sequel, as given by inspiration. we will copy, and make a few remarks thereon. In the 30th verse the Prophet gives assurance that prosperity should be to the rejoicing nation for a time ; that "the firstborn of the poor shall feed, and the needy shall lie down in safety;" but, after a time, "he shall kill thy root with famine, and slay thy remnant." This killing of the root may have reference to the killing of the two witnesses, before noticed. and the slaying of the "remnant," to the "remnant" that was affrighted. and thereby was induced to "give glory to the God of heaven." Now, what follows this admonition not to rejoice? this assurance of evil? this assurance of good to some extent amidst the evil? It is this : the dissolution of the whole nation. "Howl, O gate; cry, O city; [city of Sodom.] thou whole Palestina, art dissolved: for there shall come from the North a smoke, and none shall be alone in his appointed times." None to escape the effects of this Northern smoke ; none free from its dissolving nature. This "fiery flying serpent," like subtle smoke, enters into all departments of the nation, and the consequence is a disruption of Palestina, or the government of the land of Palestine. Thus. again, by inspiration, is shown, by different figures or symbols, the same things before noticed: and they might be multiplied from the same source : but we close for the present ; ready, however, to answer, as above, if called on.

CHAPTER TENTH.

THE Israelitish nations, as type and anti-type, correspond with the double triune form of the Godhead that produced them. Witness: The first plural form of God in attributes, of Omnipotence, Omniscience and Omnipresence, was not so clear and tangible, not so real or realizing, to our human apprehensions as was the second form, expressed by Father. Son and Holy Spirit ; so the first, or typical form of these governments. has not been so realizing as is to be their second. And again, as a full realization of the Godhead, as taught us in the Bible, is not possible, until we pass up to him by the six steps of ascent to the seventh, which alone of the whole is God, so we need not expect full realization nationally, until we arrive at or to the seventh and last head of God's ancient government on earth. This fact is further proven by the six steps of ascent to king Solomon's splendid throne, each one of which was guarded by a brace of lions; thus signifying that the nation in all its travail and labor, up to its final head, was guarded by Christ the lion. This throne figured or typed the nation in all its steps and final "throne dominion," which was not a step, but a seat. The steps were laborious,but rising higher as step by step the kingdom advanced, nearing realization, or seventh, which was not a step, but a seat; which all will see at once signified rest, no more steps of travail; "Dominion" has been obtained; the seat has been taken by David's regal son, who will sit and rule forever. To this also agrees the six labor days of creation, ending in the seventh one of rest ; for in six days were all things created, "and on the seventh God ended his work." Labor was an attitude or condition of unrest; standing and walking are common ones. Six days entire had been occupied in the work: the seventh finds the laborer in his attitude of labor—standing for instance. A degree of labor therefore is requisite on the seventh, to effect a change from standing to sitting, or one of rest; hence it is said "he finished" on the seventh. Again, upon this head: The Israelites were required to till their lands six years, and the seventh it was to rest We return, and note: That as the attributes of God are made up of various traits or lineaments, as we have elsewhere remarked, so, likewise. these governments are made up of the various State governments. which may be multiplied un til. like their great original, (God) they shall become universal, as promised so oft. A marked example or two of multiplication was given us. by God, in the dividing the tribe of Joseph into two. Ephraim and Manasseh. and of further dividing of Manassah into two. Thus was the adding of States to the Confederacy taught, and the United States did not fail to profit by the examples set; and the result was that in 84 years the States grew in number from 13 to 33. It is a patent fact that visible things tell us of the invisible : and if we understood *perfectly* the visible. we would understand and comprehend more fully the invisible, who created it. and thus be taught to "look through nature up to nature's God." St. Paul, speaking of heathen nations, or idol worshipers of "beasts, birds, and creeping things," says they were given up of God to uncleanness, because it was not an ignorance of necessity that caused them to do so. though they had not the written word. "*Because that which may be known of God is manifest in them* [the idolators] *for God hath shewed it unto them.*" How has he done it? Thus : "*For the invisible things of God ever since the creation of the world* [which is visible,] *are clearly seen.* [not dimly,] *being understood by the things that are made. Even his eternal power and Godhead" are made plain by the visible creations.* "So that they [these idol worshipers.] are without excuse," notwithstanding they had not the written word. "From" the date of creation all has been plain. if man would have given heed to the voice of creation. with the Spirit's aid. which "enlighteneth every man that cometh into the world." Creation—physical, intellectual. and political —is but the *reflex* of the mind of God, and must be like him. Creation pre-existed in the mind of God, just as the finished painting reflects but the pre-existing forms and colors of the artist's mind: *he by action simply brings them out and transfers them to canvass.* We hesitate not to say *God has mapped himself out in creation,* physically and intellectually. in families and in nations. "In families" in Noah's house ; "in nations" in Abraham's house. All the families of earth belong to the *three* families of Noah. and they are but *one* family. All the nations of earth belong, by promise. to the three nations of the fathers, and they are to be but *one* nation, and to "fill the whole earth." All others are to "become as chaff of the summer threshing floor;" "driven away, and place for them no more to be found." Geology teaches us that this globe. so far as known. is also *three in one*, or consists of three distinct formations. termed by the books Primary, Secondary, and Tertiary, or 1st. 2nd, and 3rd; and that these several formations correspond to as many periods of time. So the earth is *three* formed as to time and feature ; and from this we conclude that a government springing from the same infinite source. of form and feature, should also bear the marks of its great original. If we examine the old United States' Constitution, as well as our own. we will see the same triune feature kept up, *even* in their workings. Legislative. Judicial and Executive. Thus, we are like the Athenians, who ignorantly worshiped God, to them unknown. according to the inscription on an altar of theirs. We are ignorantly serving God, nationally, though imperfectly it be, for which we are entitled to no credit. "To God be all the glory !" who. by the influence of his Holy Spirit, directed and guided the fathers of '76 in organizing a scriptural or God like government. The same feature is repeated in all the State Governments. All governments that do not conform to this physical delineation of God. have not God for their author, and are counterfeits or corrupt, and are the offspring of fallen man, and are, as he is, averse to God ; and so. necessarily, "like begets like." This rule is changeless. All governments that hold the centralizing element in them; that tend to consolidation; that in any way favors the one man power principle, places man as *one* in the place of God. who alone is *one in power;* and as such. are at war with the Eternal and his governments on earth. and would, if possible. dethrone the Deity in heaven. Nimrod (descended from that branch of Noah's family doomed to servitude, and denied national rule. because of its groveling. sensual disposition,) was the author. as far as we are informed. of this one man power principle in governments. and established or ordered the kingdom of Babel. which resisted the decree of God to disperse. and settle wide spread. and was alone compelled to disperse by the confounding of their language. And all governments. from that day to this, that resist or in any manner hinders free and wide spread settlement or dispersion, has had, and ever will, a tendency to centralization, and are of their mother, Babel, above named, and opposed to God; and as such, must and will fail. Babel is the mother of all Monarchy. Some governments that have, or do now exist, may in some instances resemble the governments that we claim are of God, especially as to the Legislative, Judicial and Executive features named above; and so we might expect; for when there is a spurious or counterfeit thing, it must be supposed to be made in imitation of the pure, but it is only an imitation, and may pass as genuine for a time; but, when put in the crucible of God, then their drossy baseness will appear, and be rejected, and once rejected, will pass no more as genuine. All powers, nationally speaking, are in the hands of the people, in their individual capacity, aggregated, delegated to them by God; and being God's delegates, they are amenable to him alone, and not to the government they created, as his active agents. The accountability here referred to is political or national; for individual sins, in breaking any law of the land, does not involve politics, and for such sins he is most certainly answerable; the one to the whole, who is supposed to make all laws, if not in person, by representatives. The government being the creature of the people, in their aggregated capacity, cannot hold the people, in said capacity, to account; but, as the agent of the people, its duties are to carry out the will of the people: they alone have the right to "alter, change or abolish." And thus following out this self-evident and common sense view of organic governments, under one general or confederate head, we trace them in regular succession backward or up stream, to the source of right to rule. From the one government confederate, up stream to the State governments, and from these again to large communities, inorganic, and these to neighborhoods, and neighborhoods to families, and families to individuals, the springs that go to make up this great governmental river, a common figure in scripture for governments. The springs above received their power to flow into governmental form from Heaven, and should, as the rivers to the ocean return to their source, a ceaseless stream of gratitude and praise. Or, if we reverse the order and begin at the springs, (man individually,) who receives from the great source of power their origin and constant support, we trace these springs downward to creeks, creeks to larger ones, and these in turn to rivers or governments to neighborhood and governments organic to a government confederate, properly called the unum," or one made up of many. This is in strict conformity with physical nature, visibly manifested, which is but a visible manifestation of the soul itself. Witness, the great ocean, above referred to, in its various forms, ... yet many, when individualized, resembles in a remarkable degree the great source or origin of all things, even God the eternal. Witness ... of waters as one sending out itself in vapors to the visible heavens ... road, as clouds, fall in teeming showers upon the thirsty earth ... fixed, countless springs appear; (this but representing the ... organic into branches, creeks, rivers, and rivers into a river, and ... atribute to the ocean again. So, like God, it is the "Alpha and ... beginning and the ending, the first and the last;" confirming ... God had mapped himself out in creation." Who ever heard of a river ... place up stream, dividing and subdividing itself until it ended ... end of springs? The reverse of this is nature's law or order. Rivers ... make springs, but springs make rivers; continents do not make grain ... but grains of sand make continents. The whole is always made up ... sec. the parts of the whole, for that would be an impossibility ... the house is by parts; the pencilings of the artist, that ultimate in ... ing, is so likewise. The work is progressive; and so the works of God ... are progressive; not to say the same of God himself, to our ... of whose existence we could form no idea, as before shown, a definite progressive stand or starting point, and with the assistance of the spirit, the great true base up, so to speak, progressively. Again: the governments we treat of do not rest upon their lower ends, but upon the opposite ends, and resembles a tree, downward inverted, or top resting on the ground. These things being considered, how could any set of intelligent men come to the conclusion that the general government has greater powers than the State governments, upon which it is built? that the .. .. greater than the creators; or, yet again, that the States have delegated] .. .. to the general government that they could not resume at pleasure? Delegated powers, are at best but lent; not an absolute gift or bestowment, in fee simple, and farther delegated powers are always delegated to be used or exercised for the benefit of the party delegating, and not for the delegate, only so far as he may be, as a *dependent*, interested in his delegator. Some will, doubtless, object to much of the foregoing, because applicable only to a confederate form of government, since so large a portion of the earth is, and ever has been, under a different form of government, and does not conform to the physical arrangement of nature, which we assert is a physical delineation of God. But this objection does not effect our position in the least ; for we claim that all governments that *do not conform* to the physical delineation of God, are not of God, and as such, are necessarily corrupt or spurious ones.

CHAPTER ELEVENTH.

A S we have, in the lxvi ch. 8 v. of Isaiah, seen that "Zion travailed and brought forth children;" and as said prophecy has, we believe, almost universally been received as altogether spiritual, and not political, as we have treated it, for we consider it such, and not at all spiritual; and further, as offence may have thus been given to some honest children in spiritual Zion, we deem it proper to say something specifically upon this head, for be it known once for all that I am not the man to shake one stone in the fair fabric of our spiritual mother; yet I do claim that this name of the church is a *borrowed one; it is one of association.* In the year of the world 2353 the children of Israel, under the leadership of Joshua, entered the promised land of Canaan, soon drove out, killed, or subjugated its heathen inhabitants, **yet** by careful notice it will be observed that certain strongholds, one at least, **they did** not subdue, for 500 years after they entered the land. We read these facts, **1st Chronicles,** xi ch: 4 v.) "And David and all Israel went to Jerusalem, *which is Jebus*; where the Jebusites were the inhabitants of the land. And he inhabitants of Jebus said to David, Thou shalt not **come hither.** Nevertheless David took the castle [or fort,] of Zion, which is the city of David." And David said, Whosoever smiteth the Jebusites first shall be chief and captain. . . .b, the son of Zeruiah went first up, and was chief. And David dwelt in the . . . . . . here they called it the city of David." Second Samuel, Vth ch: 6th . . . c. King and his men went to Jerusalem unto the Jebusites, the inhabit- . . . which spake unto David, saying, Thou shalt not come in hither: . . . come in hither." (For they had held it against the whole . . . so it must have been strongly fortified.) "Nevertheless David . . . . of Zion : the same is the city of David." *So David dwelt in the* . . . . . of David. And David built round about from Millo . . . . strongly fortifying his city, or *fort*. as it is called by the . . . . . . This is the first time we hear of "Zion." Now say, ye that may . . . . . . stronghold, or was it the church? This place, you will . . . . . successfully defended and held for 500 years after the Israel- . . . . . . entry in general. Next, of the church: how came she to be . . . . . . be remembered that during the administration of Eli, the . . . . . . that had ever been kept in the tabernacle or tent; that had . . . . . . people in their wandering from Mount Sinai, to the time of Eli . . . . . into the hands of the Philistines; found its way, by two removals, ... Obed-Edom. Some thirteen years after David had taken the . . . . . Zion, he goes down to the house of Obed-Edom, and brings up the Ark . . . 1st Chronicles, Vth ch.: "And David made him a house in the city of David, and prepared a place for the Ark of God and pitched for it a tent, and

David gathered all" Israel together to Jerusalem, to bring up the Ark of the Lord unto his place, which he had prepared for it. . . . So David and the Elders of Israel, and the captains over thousands, went to bring up the Ark of the Covenant of the Lord out of the house of Obed-Edom with joy. . . . So they brought the Ark of God. and set it in the midst of the tent that David had pitched for it" in the city of David: thus the tabernacle or church building, so to speak, was set up in a military stronghold of the name of "Zion;" and here the nation worshiped the true God for thirty-one years, in the midst of the camp, for it was not removed from the place that David pitched for it until the temple was finished in the 11th year of Solomon's reign. How natural, then, that the name of the city of worship should be attached to its temple of worship? How very natural such expressions as "let us go up to Zion, to worship the Lord our God;" "Zion, the city of our solemnities," and hundreds of similar and kindred expressions that most certainly and explicitly refer to the church and its worship; but nevertheless the name is borrowed; its a name of association, with the military, which is but the strong arm of the civil department of the government. When the civil authorities fail, for want of strength, to execute the laws, she is directed to call on Zion the military arm, for assistance. This fort was on a hill of that name, that overlooked the city and vale of Jerusalem, and upon one end as some suppose, and others on a different but adjoining hill, was the temple built by Solomon, to which he removed the Ark; and the common name of Zion attached to the temple and the hill on which it stood. 'Tis perhaps useless to say more upon this subject; for if we should undertake to cite all of the pointed passages in which "Zion" occurs, and that evidently are spiritual, our readers would tire, for they are familiar to all christian ears; but we *warn all to be careful not to apply to spiritual Zion the one half that is said of "Zion,"* ever remembering that there are two. Of the political one Jerusalem was called the daughter, or weaker member of the government, being strictly civil. Of this Zion we should like to speak at large, but cannot do so now. We reserve for ourselves the right to do so, and shall, if any see fit to attack our position. We affirm again, most unhesitatingly, that Zion, who travailed in the 8th v., lxvi ch. of Isaiah, was and is the Confederate States of America. And before taking leave of national Zion it may be well to add something further, while the matter is in hand, and the reader's mind is upon that subject, to show that Zion, in its first or original sense, is national. Isaiah, Xth ch., the Lord calls Assyria the rod of his anger, and staff of his indignation, which he would send against Jerusalem, a hypocritical nation; saying, in the 11th v.: ' Shall I not, as I have done unto Samaria and her idols, so do to Jerusalem and her idols? Wherefore it shall come to pass, that when the Lord hath performed his whole work [of destruction,] upon *mount Zion* and on Jerusalem" that he then would punish Assyria, the nation that he had used in punishing or destroying mount Zion, or the Jewish nation. This cannot, by any forced interpretation, mean the church, for Assyria never destroyed spiritual Zion, and that too as an instrument in the hands of the Lord. He never has forsaken his spiritual Zion, but he has his national Zion ; yet not utterly, for he encourages them, in the 24th verse, saying: "O my people that dwellest in Zion, be not afraid of the Assyrian:" nation ; truly, "he shall smite thee with a rod, and shall lift up his staff against thee" as my agent to correct thee, but only for a little while, and in turn I will scourge him. "He shall shake his hand against the mount of the daughter of Zion, the hill of Jerusalem." Jerusalem was the daughter or feminine part of the nation, while Zion was the masculine or strong arm of the government. Isaiah xxix ch: 8v., the Lord mentions the disappointment of dreamers, saying. "So shall the multitude of all the nations be, that fight against mount Zion." Here a *multitude* of nations are represented as fighting against mount Zion. We have no evidence that any such multitude ever besieged the church; and in fact, we know they, as nations, never did; but on the other hand, as nations, they have ever fought against God's nationality, anciently and modernly; and it is of said nation that he here speaks, calling it "Zion." Isaiah xxx ch, God addresses his nation as rebellious children, rehearsing their evil doings, and their impotency before the pursuing enemy, saying, 17th v.: "One thousand of you shall flee at the rebuke of one'' of their enemies. He says, however, that he will wait, that he may be gracious unto them. 19th v.: "For the people shall dwell in Zion at Jerusalem : thou shalt weep no more.'' Never so said of the church on earth: her's is a perpetual warfare : wars without and fightings within are her heritage, while in the body. Her release is at death, not before; death of her individual members we mean, not in polity. Isaiah xxxi ch: 9 v., the Lord says "his fire is in Zion, and his furnace in Jerusalem." This cannot be spiritual. Isaiah xxxiii ch: 20 v.: "Look upon Zion, the city of our solemnities : thine eyes 'shall see Jerusalem a quiet habitation, a tabernacle that shall not be taken down." Zion and Jerusalem are visible realities; they are the figures of the Israelitish nation. Isaiah xxxv ch. 10 v.: "And the ransomed of the Lord shall return, and come to Zion with songs and everlasting joy upon their heads : they shall obtain joy and gladness, and sorrow and sighing shall flee away." This can never be said of spiritual Zion, for she has no such promises as this, while she is on earth. It is said "they shall *return*." Where to? we would ask. Of course to the place they had gone out from. They had gone out into political bondage ; they are here represented as coming home again: returning "to their former estate," as promised in the xvi ch. of Ezekiel. The church is not a visible but a spiritual existence, and cannot be in bondage ; can never be from home. The conscience is ever free, has no occasion to return; but in all lands and climes this kingdom is within, or it is not at all. Isaiah li ch: 2v. the nation is addressed thus : "Look unto Abraham your father, and unto Sarah that bare you : for I called him alone, and blessed him, and increased him. Hearken unto me, my people : and give ear unto me, O my nation. For the Lord shall comfort Zion : he will comfort all her waste places ; and he will make her wilderness like Eden, and her desert like the garden of the Lord." This chapter and the lii are to the point, but too long to copy. Please read them. I do not say that there are not spiritualities in these two chapters, but that in their first and most obvious sense they are national; for the reference to Abraham and Sarah as the *fleshly* origin of the nation, clearly fastens the political meaning as the first one. Jeremiah li ch: 35 v.: "The violence done to me and to my *flesh*, be upon Babylon, shall the inhabitants of Zion say." Here is a fleshly affair; that is, a curse or malediction by one nation upon another. Babylon had afflicted Israel, and Israel curses Babylon, calling the *same* to fall upon Babylon that had fallen upon them; and as Babylon was clearly a nation, which no one doubts, and must then suffer these curses as a nation; and if so, they must be political, and if political in the one case, they must of necessity be so in the other, for they were the same. Lamentations i ch: 17 v.: "Zion spreadeth forth her hands, and there is none to comfort her : the Lord hath commanded concerning Jacob [Zion,] that his adversaries shall be round about him; ' of course to afflict them. Did God ever command the enemies of the church to be round about them, to circumvent and overbrow his spiritual Zion, and that, too, while she was spreading forth her hands in supplication ? No, verily. He never did and never will ; but of national Zion this is true to the letter, and has been oft repeated. "The Lord hath . . . thrown down in his wrath the stronghold of the daughter of Judah," which daughter is Jerusalem, and which stronghold is Zion. iv ch 11 v.: "The Lord hath accomplished his fury; he hath poured out his fierce anger and hath kindled a fire in Zion, and it hath devoured the foundations thereof." Not his church certainly, but his nation that he did thus visit with destruction. Micah, iv ch., speaking of the "latter day" restoration of his nation God says, 2nd v.: "And many nations shall come and say, Come, and let us go up to the mountain [government] of the Lord, and to the house of the God of Jacob; and he will teach us of his ways, and we will walk in his paths : for the law shall go forth of Zion, and the word of the Lord from Jerusalem." "In that day, saith the Lord, will I assemble *her* that halteth, and I will gather *her* that is driven out: and *her* that I have afflicted. . . . And the Lord shall reign over *them* in mount Zion from henceforth, even forever." Here we have three personal pronouns: "*her* that halteth, *her* that is driven out, and *her* that was afflicted. They are gathered into one nation on mount Zion, and God reigns over them as one, forever. These three are the identical three in the xvi ch. of Ezekiel, called Jerusalem. Samaria and Sodom, and known to be the Israelitish nation in its divided State, but soon to be joined to never no more; and joined, are called Zion. This can in no sense be applied to the Church, for she is ever one, and never divided into three churches, more or less. 8 v., "And thou, O tower of the flock, [and further called "the stronghold of the daughter of Zion;" Jerusalem was the daughter of Zion, and Zion was the stronghold of the daughter,] "unto thee [Zion] shall it come, even the first dominion." The first dominion was Ephraim, for he was called the first born of God. Jeremiah xxxi ch, 9 v., "I am a father to Israel, and Ephraim is my, first born" nation. He has the first rule or dominion; but in the "latter day" the dominion passes into the hands of Zion, and as Ephraim's dominion was strictly a political one, and passes as such to Zion. it follows that Zion was political, by which we mean national. "Therefore they shall come and sing in the height of Zion, and shall flow together." They had been apart, but now, having flown together, they are to remain one upon mount Zion forever, while David reigns as king forever over them. In the ii Psalm God says he had set his king upon the holy hill of Zion; and that being set, he should break all nations with a 'rod of iron; should dash them in pieces as a potter's vessel. This is Christ. the king, and not Christ the great High Priest. A king sits upon a throne; a priest stands before the altar. The office of a king is to rule nations, and if need be, dash them to pieces. The office of a priest is quite different : to offer sacrifice for sins. So the person in this Psalm is Christ the king, sitting as such upon the political height of Zion, or upon the throne of Jerusalem, which is the throne of his kingly father David, and according to oft-repeated promises is never to end. xlviii Psalm, 2 v.: "Beautiful for situation, [has a locality: the church has not,] the joy of the whole earth, is mount Zion, on the sides of the north, [which is] the city of the great King." (Not the great priest.) "God is known in her palaces for a refuge. For, lo, the kings were assembled, they passed by together. They saw it, and so they marvelled ; they were troubled, and hasted away. Fear took hold upon them there, and pain, as of a woman in travail." Why all this fear, pain, travail, &c., upon the part of the assembled kings, who were political personages, on beholding the "towers of strength" and the impregnable bulwarks of Zion? Why, we say, if she was simply a spiritual existence, such haste to get away from her? She would not harm them, but do them good. Nay, she was the "city of the great king," a mighty political fabric, before whose power they quaked and "hasted away." Psalm liii, C v.: "Oh that the salvation of Israel were come out of Zion! When God bringeth back the captivity of his people, Jacob shall rejoice, and Israel shall be glad." The personalities in this passage are all national,and so must be Zion. Psalm lxix, 35 v.: "God will save Zion, and will build the cities of Judah ; that they may dwell there, and have it in possession. The seed also of his servants shall inherit it : and they that love his name shall dwell therein." Buildings, cities, possessions, &c., are local and visible things; they belong to nations and not to the church. Psalm lxxviii ch: 67 v.: "Moreover he refused the tabernacle of Joseph. and chose not the tribe of Ephraim : but chose the tribe of Judah, the mount Zion which he loved. He chose David also his servant . . . to feed Jacob his people." This is most clearly and unmistakably national; and Psalm lxxxvii is like it: "The Lord loveth the gates of Zion more than all the dwellings of Jacob. Glorious things are spoken of thee, O, city of God. And of Zion it shall be said, This and that man was born in her : and the highest himself shall establish her."

We forbear to add more, at present, as we shall have to give over, at some point, and as well here, as to add further; for our limits forbid us to say one fourth that might be said of national Zion. Of spiritual Zion it is not our purpose, in these notes, to speak; and besides, she has her untold thousands to sound her praise abroad, while political Zion has none, among all her sons, to tell us of her, so far as we know. Thus it will be seen that there are two Zions, one national and the other spiritual; two characters of Jews, one national and the other spiritual : two Jerusalems, one national and the other spiritual ; two departments to God's government, one national and the other spiritual; two natures found in his creature man, one social or national, and the other spiritual. He may be a national Jew or Israelite, who is not such spiritually. "He is not a Jew who is one outwardly; but he is a Jew who is one inwardly;" that is spiritually. "All are not Israel who are of Israel;" that is, all that are visible or national Israelites, are not spiritual Israelites. There were two circumcisions; one was "outward" and national, and the other was "inward" and spiritual: one was the "letter," the other the "spirit." The outward or national is always seized upon as a figure to illustrate the inward or invisible; the visible to make manifest the invisible. There are two heavens and earths : one national and the other spiritual ; one visible, and the other invisible. The visible or national heaven and earth are to be burned up ; the spiritual, never. The new heaven and earth promised, is strictly national, and comes in the place of those burned up. He who looks for a *literal* burning up of heaven and earth, will look in vain. The Bible teaches no such thing. The burning is political—strictly so.

CHAPTER TWELFTH.

WE will now notice a prophecy that applies to the present existing state of things in the United States, and what is soon to follow. It is recorded in the xi ch of Revelations, beginning at the 3rd verse. Mr. Baldwin has handled this prophecy ably, but has misapplied it to "Hungary." We shall follow, and copy him when he suits us, and then make our own application. "And I will give power unto my two witnesses, and they shall prophecy a thousand two hundred and three-score days, clothed in sackcloth. These are the two olive trees, and the two candlesticks standing before the God of the earth." And farther called the "two prophets," and the two "anointed ones," or the "two sons of oil." The two witnesses, two candlesticks, two olive trees, two prophets, two anointed ones or the two sons of oil, represent the same things; that is "the dual Israel of God." The two olive trees mentioned by Zechariah, (iv. ch.,) and their interpretations, as being the two anointed ones, plainly agrees with these two olive trees; for the text of Zechariah mentions two candlesticks with seven branches, and seven lamps, and the two olive trees as standing together, and representing doubly the two anointed ones. These two anointed ones plainly represent the double Israel of God ; that is, his spiritual and political Israel. The double character of God's law, and of man's nature, as a spiritual and political creature, necessitated the two kinds of government, springing from the two natures. And the double character of the Hebrew government, and the perpetual representation of this doubleness, by figurative terms, and its constant occurrence in symbols applicable alone to the people of God, is full evidence that the two witnesses represent the double character of the people of God, and can represent *nothing else*. The word prophet signifies a predictor, but means a teacher politically and spiritually, as often as it does anything else. "And when they shall be about to finish their testimony" [prophecy, or political and spiritual teachings,] "the beast" [a symbol of monarchy,] "that ascendeth out of the bottomless pit shall make war against them, and shall overcome them, and kill them. And their dead bodies shall lie in the street of the great city, which spiritually is called "Sodom and Egypt, where also our Lord was crucified." This is the same "Sodom" spiritually so named in the xvi ch. of Ezekiel, and there called a kingdom: which city and kingdom we have elsewhere shown to be Washington city, and the government it represents and gives name to. This is the only city that the Spirit has named or called Sodom, as her proper name, by which she was to be known. Those that deny the doctrines and teachings of Christ, and refuse to accept him as a Saviour, are said, in scriptural language, to "crucify him afresh, and put him to an open shame." To crucify is to kill or cause death. What has the Washington government, in the persons of its present rulers, not done to kill and totally destroy God's Israel, in Church and State? How oft have they solemnly sworn by his sacred word to do, and do not; and how often have they extorted unwilling oaths from others, that they did not intend to keep when taken? They do thus daily crucify our Lord. "And they of the people kindreds and tongues and nations shall see their dead bodies three days and an half, and shall not suffer them to be put in graves." This was a great indignity offered them, in refusing burial. It is used in scripture to represent dishonor and disregard. "And they that dwell on the earth" [a very common name for the old Roman Empire, or all Europe.] "shall rejoice over them, and make merry, and shall send gifts one to another ; because these two prophets [two witnesses] tormented them that dwelt on the earth," (Europe.) It is well known how all European monarchies rejoice at the present state of things in the new world, Let them rejoice and send gifts, for their days of rejoicing are numbered, and their last sands are in motion to their final falling from the glass of nations as monarchies. "And after three days and an half the Spirit of life from God entered into them, and they stood upon their feet ; and great fear fell upon them which saw them." "This resurrection in three days and a half is to occur about four or five years after their overthrow."—BALDWIN. They first simply stand upon their feet; which is at the end of three and a half days. How long they stood, it is not said, before "They heard a great voice from heaven saying unto them. Come up hither." A voice from heaven is a voice from God's word, who has ever, through his word, by the Spirit's agency, taught us our national duties and rights, as well as our spiritual duties and rights; and as God's double charactered Israel is here said to be dead, they both arise at the call of God, through his word, "and ascend to heaven in a cloud," or en masse, as "a great cloud of witnesses," a spontaneous, concerted movement of the heretofore dead witnesses, who in their *organic forms are one each,* and thus they are the *two witnesses ;* but individualized, they are *many,* and move as *one* cloud, not as two clouds. They did not ascend *on a cloud,* but in the *form of a cloud*—a common figure in scripture for a moving mass of people. Ascending to heaven is simply going back to the Bible, or giving heed to the voice of God's teachings, nationally and spiritually, and re-organizing their fallen government under God, and purifying their church, and acknowledging him, in the person of Christ, as king over one and high priest over the other, and forever renouncing "higher law-ism," and all the hell-isms they have heretofore been guilty of believing and teaching, which caused their death for three days and a half; chief of which is "Abolitionism." "And the *same hour* was there a great earthquake, and the tenth part [ten parts] of the city fell, and in the earthquake was slain of men seven thousand; and the *remnant* were affrighted, and gave glory to the God of heaven." Earthquakes symbolized insurrections, upheavings of the people, battles, &c. Here was evidently an insurrection followed by a bloody battle, symbolized by the slaying of seven thousand, a definite number for an indefinite one, which is of very common occurrence. And as the battle occurred the *same hour* that the witnesses, as a cloud, ascended; and as the result of the earthquake was the falling of ten parts of the city or government in which the witnesses had lain dead, it follows that the *ten parts* that fell of the nation, was the *identical cloud* that ascended. This ascension, or arising into a pure organism, as a people, necessitates their separation from the former organism, as we (the C. S.) had done before them; and that, too, before we were slain by the bloody beast. We seceded in full life; they have to secede and re-organize before they can have national life. They are first given life enough to get up and stand on their feet, and then as a cloud to mount up to national independence, through a bloody conflict, which amount s to the *fall* of the former government in ten of its States ; after which, what is left of the old city or government, are called a "remnant," who also become affrighted at their own enormities, and give glory to God, thus signifying that they will become pure, governmentally; the third and last of the three noticed before, in commenting upon the xvi ch. of Ezekiel. The reading is "the tenth part of the city fell." This we deem an error in translation ; for if only one-tenth fell, the remaining nine-tenths could not very properly be called a "remnant;" but when we consider the States now in the C. S., and ten more to secede in the great West, what would still be left behind would properly be called a "remnant." Now, as to the time of the secession of ten States in the West, we think the *humbling as* may take place as early as the 4th of September, 1864; but if not then, by adding one-seventh more of time, for Sabbaths, not counted in civil measure, and we are brought exactly to the 4th of March. 1865. Then taking Mr. Baldwin as authority for the length of time from the death of the "two witnesses," until their ascension, (we setting the time of the *death* on the 4th of March, 1861,) it will take place the last days of November, 1865; and if so, then within about thirteen months thereafter, or January, 1867, we may expect a grand exaltation of the whole nation, to its final resting place or "throne dominion;" or this last date may be the time that the "remnant" becomes affrighted, and by a re-organization of a pure government, "give glory to God," which they cannot do as a nation of corruption, as they now are. Giving glory to God *as a nation*—that is, in a national or political capacity, as such—requires first, that the government in its fundamental laws shall conform to the Bible, theocratic, confederate, states-rights republic; and being thus organized, not to disregard and trample upon the law, but to administer the same as God's agents, and not in their own rights, for "All power in heaven and earth is his." So to give glory to God *nationally*, does not require that every individual in the government should be a Christian, though most certainly this would be better, and bring unmeasured fullness of glory to God; not only politically but spiritually also. So then to become a patriot indeed, *under God*, requires that he should reign in the affections, which would always insure his reigning over the nation. We shall confidently look for ten States, in the West, to secede, and organize a theocratic, confederate, states' rights (or States sovereignty,) government, as early as the 1st of December, 1865, if not earlier; and that the then remaining States, called a "remnant," shall also re-organize, as the two preceding nations will have done: and that having thus done, the three governments, being thus alike, the two latter will confederate with the former, the C. S., and become "One nation upon the mountains (States) of Israel forever, and David shall be king over them forevermore." See xxxvii ch. Ezekiel, from the 16th verse to the end of chapter. This union upon the Confederate States, or the "new Jerusalem," we think will take place about January, 1867; but if not so early, it positively will at no very distant day; and that very soon thereafter, the "battle of the great day," or "Armageddon," will be fought by *Israel united*, as above, against the combined representatives of monarchy; and Judah being victorious, monarchy falls to rise no more, and the *millennial, confederate, states-rights republican royalty, with God in Christ as its acknowledged head and author, stands forth no longer as a promise, but a veritable and realized fact.* The "Throne of David," over all Israel, thus re-appears, and all that was promised to the house and throne of David, that was not realized in the old dispensation, will—to every jot and tittle—be fulfilled under this, the new, dispensation. In the thousand years reign that follows the peace of "Armageddon," Christ, as the kingly son and heir of his father David's throne, will reign by *representatives;* but at the ending of the thousand years his second advent occurs, and then in his *visible human person* he reigns forever on earth as a king. Then, and not until then, may we cease to pray "Thy kingdom come, ou earth." He comes the second time *without a sin offering.* He came the first time with a sin offering, and having offered it as the great High Priest, he said "it is finished!" his priestly offering was complete. "There remaineth no more sacrifice for sin." He had no occasion, on his second coming, as a king, to offer a sacrifice for sins.

CHAPTER THIRTEENTH.

CHRIST THE KING, AND HIS KINGDOM.

CHRIST is oft times called a king, and perhaps as oft called the Son of David. Why called a king, if he is no king? A king was one thing and a priest another; and very different indeed. One was the political head of the nation;

the other was the spiritual head of the church. Why was he called David's son. if not such as a king? He was too far removed,' in point of time, to be called his son by the ordinary course of generation ; and besides, it is specifically said he was "begotten of the Holy Ghost." There was not one drop of David's blood in his veins, only as it flowed through his mother ; and the genealogy was never reckoned after the mother's side of the house, but after the male side. It is said he was "David's son according to the *flesh*." Very well; that is all we claim. A flesh'ly son is simply an earthly son, in contradistinction to a heavenly or spiritual one, in which sense he was a High Priest. The kingly office is not a spiritual, but strictly an earthly or fleshly one. Christ himself refers to his sonship through David, when he asks the Pharisees "how it was that David by the spirit or spiritually, called him Lord, while yet he was called David's son ?" They could not answer him, for they would not see or receive him as either king or priest. In a spiritual sense he was David's Lord, but in an official sense he was David's son. This makes the matter quite plain to all who are willing to receive Christ as a priest and king. We say, then, that Christ was David's son officially and not otherwise. He is the son of David in the very same sense that all of his successors were, from Solomon to the last king that sat upon the throne of Jerusalem. They were all called David's sons. and were said to [sit upon] David's throne. So if the throne was David's, the king that sat upon it. was David's kingly son, though he might not have had one drop of David's blood on father or mother's side of the house, in his veins. Because it has been said "a fountain for sin and uncleanness has been opened up in the house of king David," many conclude that Christ as a priest is the son of David, for the "fountain" evidently refers to his sacrificial death—the shedding of his blood for the redemption of fallen man. All that is meant by this is that the high priest, in his personal body—not office—having been promised that in his birth he should come by a virgin and that said virgin should be of the house and lineage of David, in the tribe of Judah, and thus he came out of the loins of his father David, as promised. He could not be said to be the son of David as a priest, for St. Paul settles that point by showing that, according to the law, no priest was to be of Judah. Judah had never furnished a priest ; so David in no sense could be called a priest: and as such the father of Christ. Christ, as the son of God, was a priest ; as the son of man, he was a king. Christ, as was Melchizedek, was made a priest by God, and not according to the law. His priestly office was held outside of the regular succession, under Aaron; hence he was not David's son in this sense, yet he was in some one, and in the one we have before named ; that is, officially as a king; and as David's throne was to stand forever—not his spiritual throne, for he had none such—it follows that some one must sit upon it as his regal heir and representative, on this very earth of ours, and not in the spiritual abode of the Eternal. All of the symbols and figures of David's throne fasten it to earth, and to talk otherwise would be sheer nonsense. The throne in heaven is not David's. but God's, the Eternal. And furthermore, David's throne on this earth is also God's; and David and his successors reign but as God's representatives on earth. We will further notice the significant fact that David was anointed to the kingly office *three* different times; thus signifying that he should reign over three nations, or rather that he should have three distinct reigns ; but as he has had only two reigns, the first over the house of Judah for seven years and six months, and the second over the whole house of Israel for seventy-three years, it follows as a necessity that his regal son, somewhere in his line, should reign under his first anointing ; and as none of his kingly sons did reign under his first anointing, which was ordered by God at the hand of Samuel—for each of them reigned under his own anointing—it further follows that his kingly son Christ must and will. This specific anointing by God cannot be lost ; was not useless ; must and will be effectual. Thus the "first anointing becomes the last," and the "last king becomes first," in point of importance. This anointing sealed the covenant with the house of David as a house of kings ; it has never been abrogated or annulled, as was a former one with the house of Saul. *Saul was rejected as a king and as a house*, and David chosen and anointed in his stead, with an

15

oath *never to be broken.* "I have found David my servant: with my holy oil have I anointed him." But as he did not reign under this holy anointing, it had a further meaning than to the person David, whose father was Jesse; it had reference to "David's greater son" David, whose reign under this holy anointing, over the whole house of Israel, shall never end, as his father's did, under his two anointings by the house of Judah, and the whole house of Israel. And he who sits and reigns or rules as the head of the Confederate States of America, and guides the ship of state to and through the one thousand years of millennial reign, as the representative of Christ the great David, "is David" to all intents and purposes, no matter what may be his or their name or names, whether "John Smith" or "Billy Jones." Yet it is a little remarkable, and worthy of consideration, that the first Chief Magistrate of the "New Jerusalem" in its incipiency, should bear a name so very nearly David: Davis. Change the "s" to a "d," and you have it. Doubtless in their etemology they are the same. David broke off from the first Israel under the reign of the house of Saul, her first king, and established the first kingdom of Judah or Jerusalem. Davis broke off from the second kingdom of Israel under the reign of her first king, A. Lincoln, and established the second kingdom of Jerusalem. In seven years and six months after David left the first Israel, and organized the first Judah, th 'whole house of Israel came down to Hebron, 'his capital, and confederated with him; and he then reigned over "all Israel and Judah." In less time, and certainly within the same time after Davis left the second Israel, will the whole house of Israel come down to the capital of Jeff. Davis, and confederate with him; and then he or his successor will reign over, or administer the government over. "all Israel and Judah :" at which time, and forever after, the kingdom over all Israel will be Judah's or David's, who was of the tribe of Judah; and its inhabitants will be "Israelites." This will be the seventh and last compact, or last confederate head of the nation, and has no successor, and must remain forever.

We have passed through with the Israel of God in its six steps of ascent up to the *seat or throne,* which is the seventh, and is not a step, as were the other six. The sixth and last step brought the nation through its labor or travail to a point at which it might sit down upon the seventh elevation, as one of rest and one of rule or "dominion." Steps always indicate a forward movement; and steps of ascent are upward and onward movements, which is ever laborious, and standing; and as long as standing and moving attitudes are maintained, the journey is not finished; the goal not obtained; the nation is still in labor, until it takes its seat—a position of rest—upon the seventh and last elevation, which is not a step, but the throne to which the six steps lead. This is in strict conformity with what we have seen and said of God, who is the author of this government; and if its author, it must be like its father in some particular: and as it is impossible for it to be like God in any other particular than that, that man is as before noted, it must be like him in numbers; that is, the government is one, and only one, though we have seen that it has had *three heads,* making but *one* under the first or typical dispensation, and that it will have *three* again, under this, the realizing dispensation, in its beginning; but these *three,* as the first *three,* make but *one* and the same thing—the seventh and last compact, just as the trinity of attributes and the trinity of persons made but one and the same God, who is the seventh and last form of the Godhead. The kingdom of Israel under Ephraim is the first step in point of time and number; the same kingdom under Judah is the second step in time and number; the kingdom of Sodom, United States of America, or Manasseh, is the third in order and number, and closes the typical dispensation. Now the first settler, of the second set of threes, which set was on the West side of Jordan, strictly within the land of Canaan, was Judah, and represents himself nationally, and as he is found to be in the promised land of rest, we have a right to expect the nation he represents to ultimate in a nation of rest, *as soon as a peace is conquered.* And as said settler was the *fourth* in order of settlement and time, he is also *first* on the West side of Jordan, or in the realizing age in its beginning: and as he goes before the two remaining settlers that are to follow him, he must of necessity take the sixth step of ascent, or first as

46

to local position to the throne; for be it borne in mind that "Sodom and Samaria" are to be given unto Judah or Jerusalem for daughters. The stick of Israel, is the hands of Ephraim, is to be joined to the stick of Judah, and not the stick of Judah to Ephraim. The movement must be up to her; she must hold a higher position on the ascending steps than Ephraim or Manasseh. And as Ephraim was the second settler on the West side of Jordan, he must be the second head of the nation under the new or realizing dispensation, and as such occupy the fifth step chronologically, as well as fifth as to number; while Manasseh, still being left behind, is the third and last settler on the West side of Jordan, of the second set of threes, and must come after Ephraim, and take the fourth step as to number, but the sixth as to time. He then comes to Ephraim, and Ephraim, with his brother Manasseh, comes to Judah and becomes one with Judah, and then as one they all take the final seat upon the throne, or form the seventh or last compact of confederation. "The lion of the tribe of Judah" has guarded every step of this government, from the first to the last. It is his own. 'Tis he that at the end of the thousand years will sit upon the throne forever.

We take Solomon's splendid throne, made of ivory and gold, that was to be reached by a flight of six steps, and each step guarded by a brace of lions, to type or figure forth the kingdom of Israel in all of its steps of travel or journeyings, from its inception to final triumph or "throne dominion" under Christ the great *national redeemer* of earth. And as Judah's *national standard bore the sign of the lion*, and thus became his distinctive national mark, and made him the lion or chief tribe of the Israelitish nation, and as Christ is called "the lion of the tribe of Judah"—that is, as Judah was the *lion tribe*, Christ was the *lion* of that tribe, the chief or head of it—it follows that he is the "chief ruler" that was promised *should come* of that tribe. If being the lion tribe made Judah the head tribe, certainly Christ, being the lion of that tribe, made him the head of it *in the same sense* that Judah as a tribe was the head of the nation; and as Judah was not the spiritual head of the nation—for Levi was that—but was the political head, it follows inevitably that "the lion of the tribe of Judah " was the political head of that tribe ; and if the head of the head tribe, he certainly was of all of the tribes. And the fact that "two lions" stood upon each step of the *ascending* nation under its various heads, guarding and watching it, with a jealous eye, to final or "throne dominion;" and the further fact that "two lions" stood as guards, one on either side of the *very throne*, proves that the "lion of the tribe of Judah" has ever been with the nation, as a guard, guide and protector, and will so guard while he sits upon his throne on earth forever. The future of this throne under "the Prince of the house of David," we leave for more gifted hands to portray. I trust some Ingram, Baldwin or Cumming will take the pleasing task in hand, and burn into living lines of flame the glowing course and goal of the "Chariot throne of Christ" "whose wheels roll in fire."

'Tis high time that we, as a christian nation, should look well to our professions as such, and be careful that while we theoretically receive Christ as our spiritual head, we do not reject him as our national head. We are commanded to "kiss the Son, lest he grow angry with us, and we perish from the way ere his anger be kindled but a little." (From memory.) We are only disposed to do *half honors* to Christ, and *that* half rather theoretically than otherwise. We are professedly a christian nation, but practically we are largely deists. We in our thanksgiving orders, official reports of victories, leading state papers, &c., acknowledge, as deists, a God, but as christians who should ever "give thanks unto God the father, *through* Jesus Christ his son," we fail—fall far short of duty in this respect. We are taught in the Bible that all 'our mercies and blessings flow from God the Father *through* the Son, by and with the agency and assistance of the Spirit ; and if all blessings, then, national as well as spiritual, for we are as dependent in the one as the other, and it becomes us as a dependent nation to honestly and humbly acknowledge ourselves as such, and call upon God through Christ, for all that we need as a nation. "Christ was manifested to destroy the works of the devil;" and if national sins and iniquities, and all their consequences are not the works of the Devil, I would like some of our wise savans to inform us who is the author of them. And if there be, then, national sins or iniquities, was it not as needful that a proper offering or sacrifice be made for them, as for individual or spiritual sins? for a sin committed, remains a sin forever. No after acts of the guilty party can by possibility change its nature from sin to rightcousness; the stain remains, whether individual or national. Some agency higher than the offender must intervene before n God the offended, and the said offender, and offer satisfaction to the broken law of God, in the room of the culprit. And this we say Christ has done in a two-fold sense, corresponding to the dual or two-fold nature of man as a spiritual and political creature. That he did offer himself a willing sacrifice for the spiritual redemption of man, few will doubt in the christian land; but many, if not all, will donot the fact that he *equally so offered himself as a political or national sacrifice.* We have endeavored in a few words, in chapter second, to show that Christ was born a king; born to a political office; born as the head of the Israelitish nation. It had long before been promised that the "chief ruler"—which is nothing less than a king—should be born of Judah, and unto him should the gathering of the people be. The wise men of the East who came to seek and worship this long promised *and expected* personage, calls him "the king of the Jews," or the king of Jerusalem; and doubtless they were guided in all they said and did on this occasion by the Spirit of inspiration, and spoke a solemn truth when they said 'born king.'' And as we have shown in chapter second, that Christ was accused, arraigned, tried and executed as a political offender, and *not* accused, tried and executed for spiritual teachings, it follows that he suffered death for the crime alledged: and as the crime alledged was that of claiming to be a king in opposition to Cæsar, he then must of necessity have suffered death *as a king* at the hands of the nation. And as he so suffered, himself being without sin, he was an appropriate political sacrifice for the political iniquity of earth. There was to be "no remission without the shedding of blood," neither of political or spiritual offences; so his sacrifice was two-fold in its *nature* as it was two-fold in its *office*. As a king he dies for the national redemption of earth; as a priest, he dies for the spiritual redemption of the same. As a priest he made "his soul an offering for sin," saying in the garden, "My soul is exceeding sorrowful, even unto death." His outward man, representing the king, perhaps suffered more directly for the national redemption, as said redemption is visible and outward; and his inward man, in suffering, may perhaps be supposed to have entered more largely into the soul's redemption, as the inward in both the offender and the offering is invisible or spiritual. "The soul that sinneth it shall die," and "his soul an offering for sin" seems to say as much. God compels no man to be a spiritual follower of Christ, but has made ample provisions for all to be such, and invites them to "come." But the time is not far distant when all will be *required* to be *national christians* or followers of Christ the king; for he will, as king, "rule all nations with a rod of iron," and if need be, to subdue and bring all under his kingly rule, some must be "dashed to pieces, as a potter's vessel." God speed that happy day! All of the ancient Israelitish people were required to be genuine national Israelites, but not required to be spiritual Israelites. "All are not Israel who are of Israel," "and he is not a Jew who is one outwardly: but he is a jew who is one inwardly." That is, a man may be a Jew in a national or outward sense who is not a Jew in a spiritual or inward sense. We are *compelled* to be good citizens according to the law, but not compelled, yet invited, to be christians in a spiritual sense. The absolute requirements of the law have not been met by all citizens; but, as before stated, the time is close at hand when *sovereign force* will be brought to bear in such cases, and 'dashing to pieces" will be resorted to, if milder means fail; for "all rule and authority" must go by the board, save that of God in Christ, and Christ in his representatives, until he comes, whose right alone it is to rule. To be a good citizen requires more than to be negatively so. We must be *positively, actively* so; cannot fold our arms in listless indifference, and let matters go wrong by default, for want of a proper defense or prosecution. That false and senseless, yet common saying, that "what is every man's business is no man's business," must be ignored and set aside, and rather say, What is *any man's* business is *every man's* business; and it should be and is so in relation to national affairs, of which we are speaking. And we have a very instructive lesson upon this subject given us by inspiration, viz.: when the wicked men in the tribe of Benjamin were to be judged for their conduct toward the journeying Levite, and his concubine, and the tribe refused to give them up for judgment, then the whole nation made war upon Benjamin, and put them to the sword, *man, woman and child*, six hundred only escaping to the rock Rimmon for safety. And after this severe judgment upon the whole tribe for the sin of the few, (which sin, however, became the sin of the whole by their refusing to have them dealt with,) it was found on examination that one city had not come up to assist in the execution of the law upon Benjamin, and then the embattled host of all Israel turned their hands against that city, and slew every one, save four hundred young women; thus showing, most clearly, what was the political law of the land, that when a crime had been committed by any one, and the tribe or community in which he or they lived, refused to surrender him or them for punishment, they thereby endorse the criminal, and make *his sin their sin;* and by doing so they were made to suffer for the same, as if though they had committed it: and also showing that no man or set of men had any right to fail or refuse to come up to assist in the execution of the law against the offender : if they did, they also must suffer the same punishment due the first and second offenders. There are to be no neutrals : your neutrality or inactivity tells unmistakably on which side you belong, and you will be held to account accordingly. If you are of Israel, you must act the full part of an Israelite. He that is not on our side, is of the contrary part. "He that is not with me is against me;" "and he that gathereth not with me, scattereth abroad." We have said elsewhere that the Israelitish people made *three* distinct settlements, and at *three* distinct periods of time, in organizing their government, and that the *two* first settlements consisted of *three* tribes *each*, and that the third and last settlement consisted of *seven* tribes. We have endeavored to show the significancy of these *two first* settlements, viz : that the first settlement of three tribes on the East side of Jordan was typical or non-realizing, as they did not cross the Jordan and enter into the promised land of Canaan, and as said settlement consisted of three tribes, we must take each one of those tribes to represent a confederate head of the nation, and in the order in which they are named : Reuben, first; Gad, second; and Manasseh third; and that the character given to them was to be the character of the confederate heads that they severally represented chronologically. The *second* settlement of *three* was on the West side of Jordan, strictly *within* the land of Canaan, and thus indicates realization of the various promises of nationality ; but as they were three in number, and only *one* confederate nationality or "nation" made up of a "company of nations," was promised, (though it was oft repeated,) it follows that they each represent a confederate nationality, as the *first three did*, and also chronologically, as named in settlement:—Judah first, Ephraim second, and Manasseh third. And as there was ultimately to be but *one nation*, these three nations, represented by the three tribes, *must* unite or ultimate in one, and their *blended character* is to be the character of said nation. And as Judah was the *fourth* settler, and *first* on the *West* side of Jordan, or land of Canaan, we conclude that the *fourth* nation of that peculiar theocratic, states' right, confederate form, that should arise, would necessarily be the *first* in the realizing age, or on the West side of the great political Jordan ; and as the C. S. is the *fourth* government of that peculiar type that has arisen in the history of the world, we claim it to be the *first*, as Judah was the first in the land of promise; and if so, it is Judah or Jerusalem. It is the beginning of the realization of the promise to the fathers and patriarchs ; it is the re-appearance of the throne of David, that was to never end. Ephraim was the second settler on the West side of Jordan, so we may look for his confederate head to appear next. Manasseh is the third and last, and must follow Ephraim, as Ephraim is to follow Judah ; and they both are to be joined to Judah, and thus form the seventh or last compact.

We will now, for the first time, consider the *third* and last settlement of the children of Israel, which settlement consisted of *seven* tribes. This settlement was in the promised land of Canaan, and formed only a part of the three typical heads of the nation; and as the nation itself was typical, this settlement was also, as was the six tribal settlements that had gone before it. It could not be supposed to be without typical meaning, since all going before it are shown to be so; and if so, its anti-type must in some sense be like its type. And as the three tribes of Judah, Ephraim and Manasseh, who formed the first settlement on the *West side* of Jordan, are found to type the three confederate heads that we have named—one only of which has appeared as yet—then the question arises, Who can this settlement of *seven* type? and in what sense is it a type? We answer that it types, with an emphasis not to be mistaken, the Confederate States of America; and that it types it in number, and also in character, for the character of the C. S. has already been type by the tribe of Judah, viewed as her chronology. As we we have seen that, as Judah was the fourth settler, so the C. S. is the fourth nation in the order of nations, either form or type; hence, as the last settlement of the nation was seven Tribes or States under its typical dispensation, so in like manner its final or realizing head should appear under the same number of Tribes or States; for be it ever borne in mind that, now the settling the heads of Ephraim and Manasseh are yet to appear. They do not become *realizing under those heads*, but must be merged into, and form a part of, the nation under Judah's head, which alone is the realizing head; for, as before remarked, the promise was only one "nation and a company of nations." The stone that was cut out of the mountain without hands was to become a great mountain, and *fill the whole earth*—was to leave no room for any other nation. Her distinctive number, then, under which she was to appear was *seven*, as her typical number; and it matters not what number she may now have, or may hereafter attain to, her type could only give her birth number, her character being already given by the tribe of Judah. Now, as all agree that the Hebrew economy in Church and State *was typical*, who can object to our making this settlement and tribes typical? Is there not significancy in those three settlements of the nation as a type, both as to time and numbers, as well as to local position, or geographically? There is, evidently, a world of meaning in the first settlement of three tribes *not being in the land of Canaan*; the stormy political Jordan had yet to be encountered and crossed. We have no right to attach no importance to facts that the Spirit of inspiration has recorded in the sacred book for our "learning" as well as for our "comfort." For "All scripture is given by inspiration of God, and is profitable," &c., but how can it prove *profitable* to us, unless we give heed to its teachings upon all subjects it treats upon? So we would do well to "search the scriptures," which implies more than a casual reading of them. There is yet another significancy in this last settlement that we will notice. It is this: The nation from its beginning, to final throne dominion, was to pass through or occupy seven positions, which we have already noticed. Hence we take *each tribe*, in this last settlement, as typing a *position* severally and in the chronological order as named in the settlement: the first named to type the first step or position; the second, the second step; and so on to the seventh settler in this last settlement; and as Dan is the seventh and last settler, he will properly represent the seventh or last compact of the nation, both in character and chronologically. Does he do it? We answer that he does. He was the seventh chronologically, and thus marks the seventh head of the nation; and as this seventh head was under Judah, the character of Judah should be found in Dan, who typed him. Let us examine and see the character given to Dan, as it should correspond with Judah, who he represents. Gen. xix ch: 16 v.: "Dan shall judge his people as one of the tribes of Israel." Deuteronomy xxxiii ch: 22 v., "Dan is a lion's whelp;" and if a lion's whelp, he must be a lion in very deed. Here, as in the case of Gad, (who typed Judah under his *first* head,) we find the distinctive *lion and law-giver or judge* feature of Judah is given to Dan, while we know at the same time that Dan *never was the lion or ruling tribe; never did judge or give law to the nation.* I know it will be said that Samson, one of the judges of Israel, was of the tribe of Dan. We admit it: but that does not fill the requirement of the quotation: "Dan shall judge his people *as one of the tribes* of Israel:" *not as a man.*

Individual judges arose out of various tribes, but *only three tribes as such* ever judged Israel, and they were Judah, Ephraim and Manasseh; and all that is here said of Dan is said of him *as a tribe*, and not as to individuals, else it might be said of perhaps every tribe, that he shall judge Israel. Dan stands here as the type of Judah's final head, and all that is said of him is applicable to Judah, and to no one else—it must be placed to his credit, and his only—to Judah the great lion, law-giver and judge tribe, that gave birth to the "Lion of the tribe of Judah," who is to "rule all nations with a rod of iron." So we see this whole national settlement by settlements, and settlements by tribes, and the tribes by character and chronology, as well as by numbers, *has been typical*.

Much more might be said in argument upon this head, but we suppose enough has been said to make ourself understood, and call the attention of talented investigators to the subject, who shall be able to do it full justice, either pro or con. We do not shun or fear investigation upon any of the positions taken, or views advanced;—but rather court a thorough review and criticism,— if we have, in our ignorance, laid ourself liable to such a handling. And on the other hand, if we are correct, let those who are competent to show the facts fully —who by their character and position will command that attention that will not be accorded the unknown and unlearned—take the matter in hand. We say, let learning take the *facts*, and clothe them with a name that will give them access to all, and take the *errors* and scatter them to the four winds of heaven.

Note to Chapter Third.

FEAR lest we may be understood as saying, in Chapter Third, that man in his creation did not receive a spiritual likeness of God, we will add that he certainly did receive such a likeness, and lost it in the fall. But said likeness *"was not the very image"* of holiness, that his Maker possessed; 't was only a resemblance in point of holiness, for God in all his attributes is infinite, and man in all his is finite; and there is, strictly speaking, no comparison between that that is finite and that that is infinite. Man, after his *order*, was created *perfect*, and so far he was like God, or possessed his image of holiness, and no further.

To Publishers.

WE purpose placing our Pamphlet upon the table of every Publisher that we can have access to, through the mails. Will they reciprocate, by sending us their publications for a short time? at least such numbers as may contain any notice that they, or any one else, may think proper to give us, pro or con.

ERRATA.

PAGE 13, 21 lines from bottom, for "made" read "make;" page 7, 15 lines from bottom, for "add ho" read "and he;" page 19, 5 lines from bottom, for "Gath" read "Gad;" page 22, 5 lines from top, for "1766" read "1776;" page 23, 3 lines from top, for "maen" read "much;" page 32, 22 lines from top, for "disabled" read "dissolved." Several minor typographical errors we will not refer to, as the reader can readily detect them.

www.ingramcontent.com/pod-product-compliance
Lightning Source LLC
Chambersburg PA
CBHW031823090426
42739CB00008B/1389